Fingerprints on My Heart

How My Severely Disabled Brother Shaped My Life

HARRIET S. MOSATCHE, PH.D.

LUMINARE PRESS

WWW.LUMINAREPRESS.COM

Fingerprints on My Heart: How My Severely Disabled Brother Shaped My Life
Copyright © 2020 by Harriet S. Mosatche

Printed in the United States of America

Cover Design by Melissa K. Thomas

Luminare Press
442 Charnelton St.
Eugene, OR 97401
www.luminarepress.com

LCCN: 2020902169
ISBN: 978-1-64388-302-1

Fingerprints on My Heart

Dedication

When I received my Ph.D. in Developmental Psychology in 1977, I wrote the following in my dissertation:

> *This manuscript is dedicated to Ian Rosenberg because my interest in the field of psychology began and was nurtured because of his severe mental handicap.*

We no longer use the term "mental handicap," but I dedicate this book not only to my brother Ian, but to all those with developmental disabilities who struggle to find the respect and dignity they need and deserve.

TABLE OF CONTENTS

Acknowledgments

I THANK MY SISTER MARSHA BRODY WHO NOT ONLY PLAYED an important role in Ian's life but also read this manuscript and provided details that enriched the telling of this important story. I am very proud of my children Robert and Elizabeth Lawner who always treated Uncle Ian with love, humor, and compassion. They both offered their honest perspectives and allowed me to use their stories. From the time I met him, my husband Ivan Lawner became part of Ian's story, and I thank him for the tremendous amount of time he spent as an advocate for my brother and for reviewing the manuscript.

My writing group—Sylvia Barsion, Michele Wood, Julienne Ryan, and Cindy Babcock— deserve heartfelt thanks for their encouragement and insights over the many years it took me to take the desire to share Ian's story with the public to the actual completion of a manuscript. I need to give a special acknowledgment to Sylvia whose comments, questions, and suggested revisions of numerous versions of *Fingerprints on My Heart* were truly invaluable to me. I am deeply grateful to her for her incredibly thorough and thoughtful reviews. Having a sister with a severe disability, Sylvia understood the importance of this book.

I also acknowledge the many people whose real names can be found throughout the book who were family members or like family (Kaleigh, Rona, Marty, Uncle Hy, Sr. Romuald, Judy, Annie, Verna, and Diane) or were public figures. I gave pseudonyms to almost everyone else, regardless of whether they were saints or villains in Ian's story. But I applaud the saints and hope that the villains have become better people.

Finally, I hope this book makes a difference for the family members of people with developmental disabilities since, unfortunately, prejudice and discrimination are still pervasive. My story is one that shows the hardships of life for not only for the person with a disability but also for every member of the household. But it also depicts the positive impact of life with a family member with special needs. Not only were my career aspirations and educational goals shaped by my brother Ian but so were my compassion, patience, and assertiveness.

CHAPTER 1

Discovering the Truth

During the summer of 1960, on the cusp of adolescence, I spent my days sunbathing to look good for the cute boys at Rockaway Beach in Queens, New York, where my family was staying for three months, wondering whether any of the boys noticed me in my sleek red and white striped swimsuit and worrying about my 18-month-old brother, Ian. While cousin Judy's son, who was the same age as Ian, toddled around on the beach and spoke new words every day, Ian remained quiet—not a single word. He grunted sometimes and made a few babbling sounds, but that was it. He couldn't walk independently—one of us needed to hold his hand. It was hard not to compare the two boys.

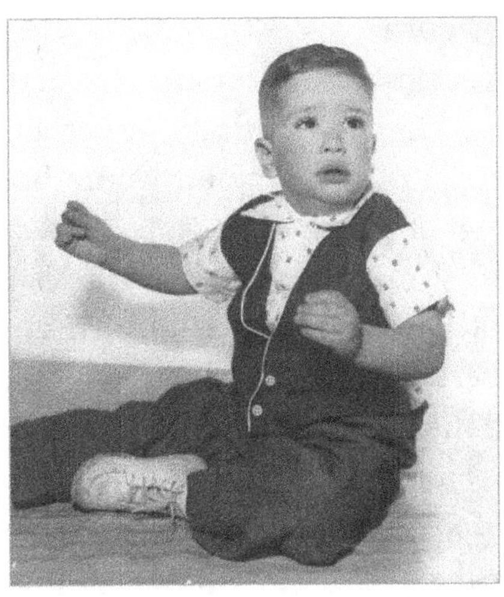

THE EARLY DAYS

When Mom learned she was pregnant with Ian in 1958, she was thrilled. My sister Marsha was already ten, I was nine, and my brother Jay was four. A couple of years after Jay's birth, my mother had suffered a miscarriage. When I learned that Mom was so happily pregnant again, I was puzzled—we were already crowded in our two-bedroom, one-bathroom apartment on the third floor of a walk-up building in Brooklyn, New York. Marsha, Jay, and Grandma shared one bedroom, and they had to walk through the other bedroom—the one where Mom, Dad, and I slept—to get to the bathroom. Not much privacy for anyone. As a very practical nine-year-old, another child just meant larger expenses and a delay moving into a bigger and better home.

But once I realized how excited Mom was about the baby growing inside her, I began to look forward to welcoming a new sibling. The birth was not an easy one, but in my family you didn't talk directly about such things. Bits and pieces of the story emerged later. It was a fifth pregnancy; labor was expected to go smoothly and fast. The doctor was late arriving at the hospital that December 24 so a nurse told Mom to cross her legs, not to let the baby come out. Even when the doctor arrived, the labor continued to drag on for hours and hours. In spite of the protracted labor, Ian appeared to be a healthy newborn.

When Mom visited her obstetrician for her first postpartum visit, he gave her a $25 gift certificate—to celebrate the birth, he explained. In the 1950's, this amount would be comparable to a $225 gift today. Later on, when Ian began to show signs of abnormal development, Mom wondered about that gift certificate, something the doctor had not given to her after the births of any of her other children. Were there signs of distress during the long labor that Mom's doctor and the nurses ignored or didn't even notice? Could Ian's brain have been injured by a lack of oxygen during the birth process? Was the doctor attempting to assuage his guilt with a gift? I will never know if something went wrong in that Brooklyn hos-

     Harriet S. Mosatche

pital on Christmas Eve 1958, but our family was changed forever following Ian's birth.

A week after Ian was born, Mom woke up with her mouth twisted on one side and her right eye closed. She thought she might have had a stroke. We lived next door to a doctor's office, so I rushed there with my mother. She almost never went anywhere alone—an agoraphobic long before the condition became popular. Mom was diagnosed with Bell's Palsy, which most people recover from. Not Mom. Her mouth stayed twisted. She lost vision in her right eye and it shed tears constantly. "That's what happens in our family" became our motto when worst-case scenarios became the reality. But Mom ignored her physical distress so she could focus on the four children who needed her, including a helpless newborn.

CHANGES—A MOVE, ILLNESS, AND HYPERACTIVITY

When Ian was seven months old, Mom and Dad borrowed money from relatives for the two thousand dollar down payment on a house in a safe neighborhood in Brooklyn with good public schools. We moved from our cramped apartment into a private home with three bedrooms upstairs, a den on the first floor (which was turned into a bedroom for Grandma), and a basement—a palace for our family. The day we moved in, I kissed the stairs going up to my bedroom—I was grateful to have a room I only had to share with Marsha. We continued to live frugally—eating spaghetti covered with ketchup as our version of pasta with marinara sauce and dining on salads of iceberg lettuce and carrots mixed with a bit of vegetable oil and Kosher salt.

Ian slept and ate well during his first year and met the established benchmarks for rolling over and sitting up. When he was awake he seemed alert and cheerful, although not particularly curious. People often commented on what a good baby Ian was. A neighbor used the term "placid" to describe his temperament. The photos from that time show a beautiful child with long, thick eyelashes. Around his first birthday, Ian developed a stubborn intestinal illness and took antibiotics for more than a year. Before his illness, he had said his first word, "mama," but afterwards, he stopped talking.

By Ian's third birthday, his intestinal condition had finally subsided, but it was obvious that he was not developing normally. Dad reminded us that Albert Einstein was slow as a child, and he turned out to be a genius. Although Ian could run and was toilet-trained, he did not speak, and complicated commands baffled him. However, one day he suddenly said: "Good-bye daddy" as my father walked down the kitchen steps to the side door to leave for work. Shocked, Dad asked: "What did you say, Ian?" "Good-bye daddy," Ian repeated. We all jumped for joy. Ian could talk. But that was the only phrase Ian ever said. He never spoke again.

Once a calm infant, Ian became a hyperactive toddler, one who slept little and moved constantly, often aimlessly. His pediatrician, however, was reassuring. "Maybe he won't go to college, but there's nothing wrong with him." My parents weren't convinced and took Ian to Brooklyn Jewish Hospital for an evaluation. Doctors there recommended Thorazine to address his behavioral issues, the first of many drugs prescribed to reduce Ian's hyperactivity. The definition of mental retardation, the term used most widely at that time, had been created by the American Association on Mental Deficiency and was defined as: "subaverage general intellectual functioning, which originates in the developmental period and is associated with impairment in adaptive behavior." The conclusion of the assessment was that three-year old Ian did not meet the criteria of mental retardation but rather had "average or borderline intelligence."

MY RELATIONSHIP WITH MOM AND DAD

While Marsha, Jay, and I were in school, Mom did her best to keep Ian busy and prevent him from destroying the house. By the age of four, Ian was constantly running around the house, pulling on everything he could reach and fighting off efforts to keep him in one place for more than a couple of seconds. Nothing on the kitchen table or in bedroom closets was safe. Ian was fast—in the blink of an eye, he could grab a dish from the table or pull a dress down from a closet when the door was left slightly ajar.

Dad worked two jobs six days a week to make ends meet, and when he was home, he slept. He was a champion sleeper—the telephone ringing, kids running up and down the stairs, Ian grunting when he wasn't happy—Dad just kept right on sleeping. He had learned to do that in the Army. He often talked about serving in the Pacific during World War II, not about the gruesome stuff, just lighthearted stories like when he shot a tree limb that refused to "halt" its rustling in the dark as Dad had commanded. In the Army, Dad knew that when he had a chance to rest, he'd better do so since he had to be on high alert when he was awake. When we needed Dad's help with Ian, we sometimes had to shake him into consciousness.

Although Dad worked long hours in Manhattan, he managed to arrange special times occasionally for just him and me. Once, we went to the Brooklyn Children's Museum during Passover for an Easter egg hunt. Some of the eggs I found were candy ones. Although my family followed a strict Kosher for Passover rule, Dad said: "Go ahead, eat them, but don't tell Grandma." Those candy eggs were the perfect dessert after the chicken fat on matzoh sandwiches—cholesterol heaven—we had brought with us for our lunch.

Since Dad wasn't available to spend much time with Ian, Marsha and I did as much as we could to help Mom out. When we were home from school and didn't have too much homework or during weekends or summer vacation, we strapped Ian in his stroller and went for long walks. When we stopped moving—maybe waiting for the traffic light to turn green—Ian grunted and pulled at the stroller wheels or at our jackets. It was his way of telling us to "get moving."

I valued the times when Mom and I walked with Ian secure in his stroller since we had a chance to talk— about a stuck-up girl in my class, my latest crush, maybe a bit of gossip about her cousin's fight with her husband. I loved those conversations—Mom was a great listener. Sometimes, I wheeled Ian up and down our street by myself, allowing Mom time to chat for a few minutes with a neighbor. As Ian got bigger but still willing to sit in his stroller, people often stared at him and at us. Although he had an engaging smile, his grunts sounded threatening to those who didn't know him. And when he was frustrated, which happened when he wasn't understood or couldn't do something, he grabbed anyone close by. Grunting and grabbing were Ian's main forms of communicating that he wanted something—attention, a different song, or a snack he had just spotted.

Harriet S. Mosatche

CHAPTER 2

School, Friends, Family, and Twine

Doctors tried a variety of drugs to reduce Ian's hyperactivity, but they either had no effect or even worse increased his energy level. Getting him to quiet down and go to sleep was an ordeal. But Marsha and I found one technique that worked—reading Dr. Seuss books aloud to him. We read them over and over until Ian fell asleep. I can still recite long passages by heart from many of the books. Other times, Marsha and I would just catch up on what was going on in our lives, hoping our quiet voices would lull him to sleep—we knew Ian wouldn't be able to repeat anything we said. When we heard the even breathing that meant sleep, we would quietly tiptoe out of the bedroom that Ian shared with Jay. On occasion, we were wrong, and by the time we reached the door, Ian would be sitting upright and making noises and we had to start talking or reading aloud again.

MY LIFE AT SCHOOL AND CAREER ASPIRATIONS

Although my home life centered on Ian, school was always very important to me. In my junior high school, girls and boys had separate Shop classes. Girls received instruction in Home Nursing, Sewing, Cooking, and Novelty (also known as "Learn to Make Stuffed Animals and Knit Squares for Afghans"). Regardless of our interests or talents, girls were not permitted to take courses like

Woodworking or Cars—this was in the early 1960's when treating male and female students differently was still officially sanctioned. In Home Nursing, I learned to make a bed with hospital corners while a patient (a classmate) was lying in it. Decades later, I am still waiting to use what we were told was a vital skill. One of my most embarrassing experiences was receiving the award at a school assembly for being the top Novelty student. Why would I ever want to be seen by my classmates as an expert in what I considered "old-lady" skills?

Our coed classes included the usual Math, Science, Social Studies, and English, but also Career Guidance and Library. The latter two had the reputation for being totally useless, and Marsha confirmed that fact, having taken those classes the previous year. When I heard about an opportunity to work during those periods in Mr. G's Special Education class (mainstreaming of children with special needs would not become part of the school system until many years later), I quickly signed on. I could do something useful rather than be tortured learning about the Dewey Decimal system and a possible future career as a Novelty teacher. I didn't know many women who had careers. Of the few women I knew who had jobs, none had careers I might aspire to. My mother's cousin was a secretary in a law office and an aunt held a clerical job in an insurance company. I did have an aunt on my father's side who was a psychiatrist, but I barely knew her since she lived in Ohio and her existence was a closely guarded family secret. She wasn't Jewish and my grandmother's rabbi had told my uncle not to reveal to his mother that he had married a "gentile." "It would kill her," the rabbi cautioned.

Besides, I had decided what I was going to do when I was five—right after I dropped out of school for a few days. I planned to become a Kindergarten teacher, a totally fair and caring one. Although my Kindergarten teacher Miss Davis was typically kind, one incident changed my opinion of her. My classmate Stephanie and I were playing a game when Miss Davis told the class we had

    Harriet S. Mosatche

three minutes to clean up. Stephanie was so methodical about getting each piece into the right slot in the box that we were running out of time. "Hurry, Stephanie. Just get everything into the box."

"Harriet, we have to do it right," she insisted. When our teacher rang her bell, we were still scrambling to finish putting the pieces away. Miss Davis told us how disappointed she was in us. "It's Stephanie's fault," I thought, but I didn't utter a word in my defense. I was the girl who was afraid to raise her hand to ask to use the bathroom. Was I going to argue with a teacher about a scolding? The next morning I told Mom that I had learned enough in school and didn't need to go back. Mom allowed me to stay home until I was ready to return, and after three days I resumed my formal education. Thus began my quietly assertive approach to make schooling meet my needs.

Eventually, that included deciding to work with Special Ed students for a year while my classmates were taking Library and Career Guidance classes in junior high. Getting to know Ricky (who had facial disfigurement as well as significant brain damage as a result of being dropped on his head by a nurse shortly after his birth) and the other students was heartbreaking—it reminded me of what was probably in store for Ian. Things weren't so bad while the Special Ed students were in their classroom, but when they left the school building to get to their bus, they were teased mercilessly. Words like "retard," "moron," and "idiot" were slung at these students. I said nothing to the bullies nor to the victims, too shy to do what was right. Besides, saying something might betray my secret—that I had a brother who was like them. To this day, I have a visceral reaction when anyone says "Retard" or "That's retarded." Only now I have the courage to speak out.

In addition to teaching this special education class, Mr. G also led a three-day school outing to Washington, DC, open to all junior high school students. It took more than a year of babysitting to save up the $67.50 fee, but I loved every minute of that trip and didn't even mind Mr. G telling us on the bus trip back home that we were the worst-behaved group he had ever taken to DC. I had just spent three days as a normal teenager, rarely thinking about Ian.

As a shy teenager, I never raised my hand in my junior high classes and hardly ever in high school. "Your daughter is very smart," teachers repeatedly told my parents, "but she needs to express herself more in class." Although I was quiet in class, I had no problem making friends. I had a knack for listening, understanding different viewpoints, and showing compassion. Making and keeping friends came easily to me. But, because of Ian, I usually went to their houses or played with them outside.

Only one friend became a regular visitor to our house. Maybe it was because Nancy had family problems too—her father had died when she was three, and she lived in a run-down apartment with her mom—so I felt comfortable sharing my family situation with her. She had a Chihuahua, which she often brought to our house. I was a little afraid that Ian would grab the tiny dog, but I watched him and the dog carefully to make sure they kept their distance from each other. I was relieved and grateful that Nancy accepted Ian. But when we were in junior high, she made a comment that changed everything. "You feel about Ian the way I feel about my dog. They're the same. Ian is more like a dog than a person." Nancy's words stabbed me. She didn't understand. I wanted Nancy to recognize and appreciate Ian's laughter when he observed a slapstick fall, his way of showing affection with a gentle touch, his ability to discern a new hairdo or pair of eyeglasses. "He's human, he understands so much" I wanted to say, but I kept quiet. I couldn't afford to lose a friend who knew about Ian and continued to come over to play. But our friendship was limited by the way I now knew she viewed Ian.

Extended family members and friends sometimes visited, but most were uncomfortable when they heard Ian make strange noises or when he grabbed objects off the kitchen table and threw them to the floor. Each time I've seen the portrayal of the young Helen Keller in *The Miracle Worker* movie or play, I'm reminded of young Ian. Like Helen's mother, my mother had a hard time disciplining

     Harriet S. Mosatche

Ian. "He has more than enough to deal with," she'd explain. Unfortunately, no Annie Sullivan ever entered our lives to save the day. When we had company, one of my parents or Marsha or I would usually take Ian upstairs to entertain him or put him in his stroller for a walk so that the rest of the family could enjoy their conversation. One uncle, a psychiatrist (who should have known better), asked us, "Aren't you embarrassed to have your friends over here?" I wasn't sure what he wanted my parents to do with Ian or what he wanted our answer to be. Yes, it was certainly hard to have friends over, but what was the alternative?

A GROWING REALIZATION

Gradually, each family member came to admit that Ian was "mentally retarded," the term I intensely disliked but one that was the norm back then. Nowadays, his condition would be considered a developmental or intellectual disability. My parents thought Ian would benefit from being with others who had similar disabilities. But Ian seemed different from the students in Mr. G's Special Education class. He was adorable with an award-winning smile, but he was also hyperactive and destructive—smashing dishes left on the table and throwing containers out of the refrigerator. During the summer of 1963, a Y day camp accepted then four-year-old Ian into its special program, but only if Marsha and I "volunteered" to help out. We agreed—anything to get Ian into an organized program where he could learn to interact with peers and allow Mom a bit of a respite.

The camp director placed me in the group led by Bob who was sweet and cute—an adolescent's dream. I bored Marsha on the bus ride home with details about Bob's every word and action, how caring he was to the kids. Marsha, unfortunately, was assigned to the group Ian was in. For her, it was worse than staying at home with him since she had to be extra careful that Ian didn't grab someone who did something that disturbed him, such as whistling an unfamiliar tune or standing too close.

At the end of the first week, the camp held a barbecue, inviting family members to join the campers and staff. Ian wouldn't let Mom out of his sight. She had to prevent him from pinching a nearby camper or grabbing a counselor's eyeglasses when one came by to offer a friendly greeting. Mom did not put on her happy face that afternoon. When Bob asked her whether Ian had eaten anything, she replied, "He's eating my heart out." I cringed. How could she answer that way in front of my crush? Why would she show her frustration now?

During the second week of camp, Ian's group took a field trip to the firehouse. The men helped the kids climb up on the fire truck to show them the equipment. Most of the kids were quiet and cooperative, but not Ian. He grabbed one fire fighter's hat and reached out to pull his hair. Marsha found it difficult to ply Ian's fingers away as he pinched the man's upper arm. The fire fighters were not fazed by Ian's behavior. They were used to physical dangers. But Marsha couldn't wait for the trip to end. Aside from some initial embarrassment about Ian and guilt about the relief that I experienced when Marsha, and not I, had been selected to work with Ian's group, I had enjoyed the two weeks of camp. Not Marsha—she admitted that the two weeks felt like two long months to her.

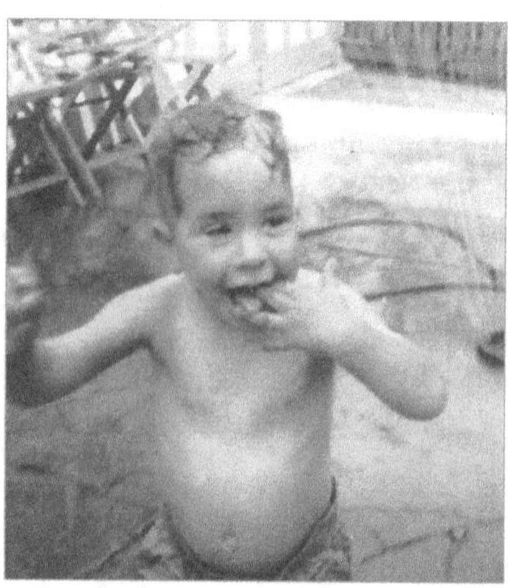

        Harriet S. Mosatche

MAGICAL SUBSTANCES

The summer was easier for us than the other seasons because Ian seemed content to spend time in the baby pool in our backyard. With a washcloth, Ian dripped water on himself over and over again, sometimes for an hour or more, until his fingers were shriveled and he began to turn blue with cold. During those times, Mom often took out her knitting. She sat and watched Ian while her fingers rapidly moved those needles around the wool. Although we didn't have air-conditioning at home, we didn't mind the heat so much since it meant that Ian was able to entertain himself outside in the water or in the tiny sandbox my parents had placed in the backyard. Ian picked up handfuls of sand, allowing the grains to flow through his fingers, an action he repeated until sand got in his eyes or it was time for him to eat.

Unraveling twine was an all-season activity for Ian who became a machine with that twine. Within two minutes, he could unravel a thick piece, but we had to ration the twine since it was expensive. Friends and relatives gave us any twine they found, knowing it was a life-saver for us. Ian's hands became calloused from handling that rough material, but the activity calmed him. Neighborhood kids sometimes laughed at Ian working on his twine, but Ian didn't seem to understand that they were insulting him when they said: "Look at what that crazy kid's doing." We swept up the remnants after Ian's unraveling sessions on the front stoop, but no matter how good a job we did, we found twine threads in the laundry, in a kitchen cabinet, sometimes even in our hair or underwear.

CHAPTER 3

Going to Extremes

As a junior high and high school student I didn't pay much attention to news stories, but I was interested when a 1962 report from President Kennedy's Committee on Mental Retardation concluded that "…we as a nation have for too long postponed an intensive search for solutions for the problems of the mentally retarded. That failure should be corrected."

THE POLITICAL AND SOCIAL REALITY OF THE 1960'S

In 1963, President Kennedy signed the Mental Retardation and Community Mental Health Center Construction Act and addressed Congress about the need to reduce the number of people confined to institutions. After President Kennedy was assassinated in 1963, his brother Robert championed the need for more humane care for individuals with retardation. I knew that part of the reason for the Kennedys' interest in care for people with developmental disabilities was that their sister Rosemary was mentally retarded. I learned that, similar to what had happened to my mother, Rose Kennedy was told by a nurse to keep her legs crossed because the doctor was not available to deliver the baby. But unlike what happened in my family, the Kennedys' money allowed Rosemary a more comfortable existence with private tutors and boarding schools, a sharp contrast to state institutions like Willowbrook on Staten Island. When Robert Kennedy visited Willowbrook in 1965, he called it "a snake pit," but his words never gained traction with the public, and conditions

   Harriet S. Mosatche

remained deplorable there for many more years.

The reality was that in 1964, when Ian was five, there were few options for those with significant disabilities. Some schools had Special Education classes, but the federal law, now known as the Individuals with Disabilities Education Act (IDEA), which mandated individualized program plans for children with disabilities, wasn't passed until 1975. Translation: schools could easily avoid enrolling Ian. Mom and Dad had finished their education at the high school level. They were intimidated by those in authority, so they passively accepted each school's refusal to enroll Ian. Administrators explained: "No, we can't deal with a mentally retarded child who also has behavior problems" or "We don't accept students who are mentally retarded—we only teach those who are emotionally disturbed."

FROM THE HORRIFIC TO THE EXEMPLARY

After numerous refusals, a small private school accepted Ian as a student. Three days into Ian's schooling, he came home with horrible red and purple bruises all over his body. I cried when I saw those injuries. Ian's pediatrician identified the marks as burns, like those made from being tied with a rope. My distraught mother called the school. "What happened?" she asked the director.

"We couldn't control Ian, so we tied him up." The director didn't apologize or make excuses, as if those actions were an acceptable method of discipline. The friction burns were caused by Ian trying for hours to get out of the restraints. No one intervened, no one rescued Ian from the abuse. and no one called my parents to pick him up early. My parents sought advice from one lawyer after another, hoping to get financial compensation for the trauma Ian had endured, maybe enough to pay for a different school. They had clear evidence of official wrongdoing and inhumane treatment, even a letter from a pediatrician indicating that Ian had suffered friction burns, likely made by a rope tied all around him—even around his groin causing swelling of his testicles. Yet each lawyer proved to be unable to get results. Ian regressed; he was no longer toilet-trained and for a year after that horrific experience, he often woke screaming during the night, perhaps from nightmares in which he relived the terrifying ordeal of that school day. Although my parents did not have an alternative placement, they knew they could not return Ian to that horrific school.

My parents continued to search for a school or program that would accept Ian. Our neighbors on the street, largely Italian and Irish, all Catholic, went to a nearby church and told my parents about a program on Saturday mornings for kids who were mentally retarded. Although our family was Jewish, Sister Romuald became our salvation and should have been made a saint. She recruited a group of older teens to work with children like Ian. While every other institution had turned Ian away, this program run by a nun welcomed him. It didn't matter that Ian was hyperactive, destructive, and nonverbal. He was one of God's children, according to Sister Romuald, and he would be cared for every Saturday for two hours. Two hours of freedom, time for the rest of us to be together.

After dropping Ian off at the St. Thomas program at 11 AM, we went to a nearby luncheonette for an early lunch. The owner could not have understood how wonderful it was for us to have a conversation without being distracted by a knocked over water glass or eating without needing to protect the contents of our plates from grabbing hands. We didn't eat breakfast those mornings, so we were starving when we arrived at the luncheonette. We listened attentively to the list of special sandwiches. Everything was delicious, and we didn't talk about Ian.

When Sister Romuald recognized the positive impact of her program on Ian, she added a two-hour private therapy session during the week. Sister Romuald's program and therapy lasted for only a year because she got sick. Cancer, we later learned, that had spread quickly. She was dead six months after her diagnosis. A tremendous loss for her family and St. Thomas, but a tragedy for us, too.

	Harriet S. Mosatche

KEEPING IAN SAFE

Soon after Sister Romuald's death, I watched a news story on television about a total solar eclipse that would occur in a week. Warnings filled the air waves about the blindness that would strike anyone foolish enough to stare at the sun. Even just glancing at the eclipse through a window could cause eye damage. Although my parents said they would keep Ian inside the house, I wasn't convinced that doing so was enough to guarantee Ian's safety. "We'll keep the blinds closed," Mom promised, as if Ian wouldn't push them away as an act of spontaneous disobedience. I could imagine him laughing as he did that and then never seeing again.

But I had a plan. Mom, Dad, and Grandma could stay on the main floor of our house, while my brother Jay and I would take Ian down to the basement. But even that wasn't enough protection. Although the basement was largely underground, there were small windows just below the ceiling. Ian might dart over to one of them and look up to the outside. So I decided to take Ian into the tiny room that contained the oil tank, the one room in the house without windows. In addition to the oil tank, there was a jumbo storage trunk containing old photos, cartons of out-of-season clothing, and just enough room for Ian, Jay (if he agreed to the plan) and me to squeeze in.

After I described the danger of the solar eclipse to Jay, he was convinced that spending a couple of hours in that cramped space was the only surefire way to keep Ian safe. Marsha was relieved that we had a plan since she would be away at the time of the eclipse and couldn't help out. As we led Ian down to the basement the day of the eclipse, we told him we were going on an adventure. We brought lots of supplies with us—snacks, water, and Dr. Seuss books. I had done my research and knew exactly when the dangerous period would begin and end. We entered our bunker 30 minutes early, just to be absolutely sure that scientists hadn't miscalculated the time of the eclipse, and came out two hours later, long after Dad had called to us to say that it was safe to return upstairs. During that time in the bunker, Jay and I took turns reading and singing to Ian, giving him snacks, and reminding him that this was a very special adventure just for the three of us. Later, hearing about cases of individuals who had lost their vision because they hadn't heeded the warnings, we knew we had done our job of keeping Ian safe. Years later, Jay and I admitted that our actions might have been a bit extreme. In fact, we often laughed when we talked about our time in the bunker. But in our family, we felt we could never be too careful.

CHAPTER 4

Formal Education and the Promise of Patterning

The search for a school or a professional who could help Ian was a never-ending challenge throughout Ian's childhood. As he got older, he became more and more difficult to control. Ian had more energy than any child we'd ever seen, and it was energy that no one knew how to channel. One moment he was running through the living room, and the next he was throwing a carton of eggs on the kitchen floor.

FROM THE TRADITIONAL TO THE RADICAL

When Ian was seven, the New York City Board of Education agreed to send over a teacher's aide, who was supposed to work with Ian for a few hours three times a week. The reality was that she came once or twice a week, didn't stay for more than two hours at a time, and spent almost none of that time with Ian. Instead, she helped with a bit of the housework or chatted with Grandma, who was happy to have someone to talk with. None of Grandma's sisters lived nearby any longer—since the move to our house, they were a train and bus ride away—and Grandma never made friends in our new neighborhood. After a few months, it became clear to our family and to the Board of Education that this arrangement was not working, so Ian's formal "education" stopped and was never resumed.

Mom and Dad latched onto any idea they heard about—anything to help Ian. Friends, relatives, and news stories offered all kinds of possibilities. One place in Chester, Pennsylvania offered hope through an innovative new program for children with brain injuries. Those who couldn't speak learned to speak, those who couldn't walk started to walk. Reputable magazines described this form of therapy that created new brain patterns. The regimen was one that would be difficult to adhere to, but we were determined to do whatever was needed for Ian. Now we had to get Ian accepted into the program.

Because we didn't have a car (nor did Mom or Dad know how to drive anyway), we had to recruit a relative or friend who could provide the transportation to Chester for Ian's evaluation. Although most of the work would happen at home, we would have to make trips every couple of months to the program center for assessments and program revisions. Uncle Hy, Dad's brother, said he would drive us to the initial appointment—back and forth in one day—even if there was only a slim possibility that Ian could improve. The evaluation consisted of lengthy interviews delving into Ian's birth, infancy, and early childhood and an examination of Ian's physical and cognitive skills. It was worth the trip: Ian was accepted into the program at the age of eight, young enough to benefit from this intervention. I was very happy and optimistic.

THE EQUIPMENT AND THE RULES

Our first step was to gather materials and put together a "crawl box." My parents were not handy—that's putting it mildly. If something needed a minor repair, it required a major overhaul after Mom or Dad attempted to fix it. Our neighbor Carl, a police officer, along with a couple of his buddies, offered to make the box—it was about 10 feet long and only a couple of feet high with an open top that would be crisscrossed with rope. Ian had to crawl through this box multiple times each day—no holidays, no breaks, we were instructed. The dining room table was pushed to the side and

     Harriet S. Mosatche

the crawl box became a key piece of furniture for Ian's care. The behavioral psychologist B. F. Skinner would have been proud of us as we used small snacks—positive reinforcements as he called them—to entice Ian to keep crawling through that lengthy box. When I met the renowned Dr. Skinner years later at a party at a psychology conference, I sat just two seats away from him, but my still-shy self never told him about the important role he had played in our family's life.

We also needed a "patterning" table, something like a massage table. Carl and his friends made this one, too, with a washable bright orange vinyl surface. It was placed in the kitchen nook that once contained our kitchen table. We needed to find five people for each patterning session, and five five-minute sessions were required each day. Ian was placed on his abdomen on top of the table. One person was responsible for turning his head, and one for each arm and leg, putting Ian in a position that resembled crawling in place. And it all had to be synchronized—one, two, three, turn the body part you're assigned to; one, two, three, turn. Over and over until the timer rang and the five minutes were over. The neighbors often stayed to chat before we agreed about the timing of the next session. Ian was in this program for three years, long enough for me to start college. No hanging out in the library or the coffee house after classes—I had to rush home to be on time for a patterning session so I could relieve Mary, Ellen, or Valerie, my mom's best friends who all lived on our street. Although I sometimes thought about how much I would have enjoyed going away to college and wished my family life could be more normal, I pushed those thoughts away. More than anything, I wanted to help Ian and I loved him, even when I resented him. I did have friends at college, but they never came over. Too much to explain. Too much noise. Too much of a mess.

On weekends, the men on our street were home, and they came by for patterning sessions. Kevin, a barber, with his Irish lilt, Carl, the cop, Ryan, the construction worker—they all learned what they had to do. They didn't talk much while waiting for the others to show up. They were there to do the patterning and go back home to watch TV or make home repairs, except for Kevin who stayed to tell stories or to hear Dad sing *When Irish Eyes Are Smiling*, which was Dad's favorite song for some unknown reason.

The salt baths were the most painful part of the program—both for Ian to endure and for us to administer. It sounds abusive—taking a washcloth dipped into a thick salt paste and rubbing Ian's body with it. But that's what the doctors ordered us to do, and we were committed to following the instructions. The theory, as I understood it, was to provide extra sensory stimulation that would waken parts of Ian's brain that weren't functioning well. Mom, Dad, Marsha, and I worked in pairs on Ian, distracting him and restraining him so he wouldn't grab the washcloth or put the salt mixture in his mouth or in his eyes.

Other parts of the program were easier. Having Ian pick out particular coins—a quarter, a penny, a dime—from a pail without looking. Getting Ian to place blocks of different shapes into a puzzle box. Then there was something like an oxygen mask, which we had to place on Ian's face a few times a day. It sounds like torture, but Ian got used to all of these activities and sometimes seemed to cooperate just to get them done and get his snack. All the time we were getting Ian to go through the crawl box or pick out coins or sit in a salt bath, we were talking to Ian, praising him. Over and over and over again.

DRIVING ADVENTURES

Every couple of months, we made the trip to Pennsylvania so that Ian's progress could be assessed and perhaps a new exercise added to his regimen. Most of the time, it was Uncle Hy who drove. A GPS or even MapQuest directions would have helped, but neither existed in the late 1960's. Uncle Hy had the worst sense of direction, and he knew it. But he did have a great sense of humor and the patience of a saint. Sometimes, it took a while before anyone knew we were lost. Navigation wasn't a strong suit in our family. Once, at

 Harriet S. Mosatche

a stoplight, Uncle Hy asked for help from another driver in getting back to the right highway—the one we had somehow missed. The man indicated that we should follow him. And that's what we did, for at least 15 minutes. He took us up and down winding roads and then pulled into a driveway somewhere in rural Pennsylvania. It was at that point that it finally dawned on us that the driver must have motioned for us to make a turn earlier. Instead, we just kept following him, wondering why we still weren't on a familiar highway. Uncle Hy didn't seem distressed. He had us all laughing about how he thought that the nice man wanted us to meet his wife and maybe even have us over for afternoon tea. Somehow, we managed to get to our destination and back each time, with a few detours and an adventure or two.

Not wanting to take advantage of Uncle Hy's kind offers of help, my parents asked others to drive them to Pennsylvania from time to time. Two of my cousins volunteered. As new drivers, they welcomed the opportunity for long-distance driving. And then there was my father's friend Henry, who drove us once. Someone could write a book about Henry, a man who seemed to have had many occupations, but what was true and what was not was hard to figure out. All I know was that he gave my father silk scarves designed with insignia representing the famous New York restaurant, the 21 Club. Henry told my dad that he was a chef at the restaurant, but more likely he was a busboy or maybe the coat check person. I don't know how he got those scarves, but we had enough to provide one to most of the female relatives in our large extended family. At other times, Henry said he was a professor at Hunter College. But Marsha attended that school and couldn't find a faculty member with that name. Whoever he really was remained a mystery, but he was caring enough to spend a day driving Ian and my parents to Pennsylvania and refused to take any money for doing so.

CHAPTER 5

A Night of Romance, A Day in Hell

While our focus on Ian was a central part of my family's life, from time to time other events grabbed the spotlight. When Doris, my high school friend, held a backyard party just before college began, she was thoughtful enough to not only invite me but also asked Marsha to attend.

A FATEFUL PARTY

We both got dressed up in our Hippie stylish bell-bottom jeans with flowing, fringed blouses and walked the block over to Doris' house. I was excited about meeting new people, particularly guys. Shy as I was, something about that evening felt different. As each new guy came over to talk, my confidence grew. Alan approached me, and as soon as he told me about his band, his attractiveness grew markedly. While not exactly one of the Beatles, his band had performed in the well-known Town Hall in Manhattan, and he was going to Brooklyn College in the fall, like me. We stepped over the almost invisible wire that separated the concrete from a grassy area and sat down to continue our conversation. I must admit that I had lost track of Marsha. I was living out a dream and had no interest in finding out whether my sister was having a good time. Suddenly, a collective gasp was heard—Marsha had tripped over the wire, trying to get to the area where Alan and I were sitting, and fallen. She quickly got up, and I ran over to her to make sure she was okay. "I'm fine," she said. "I'm going home. I just wanted to let you know that."

"I'll walk you home." I was going to assure Alan that I would be back in just 10 minutes.

But Marsha said, "No, I'm okay, I'm going home now and I don't need you to go with me."

Marsha seemed okay, but her tone was angry. I asked again: "Are you sure you don't want me to go with you?"

"No." She held her left arm stiffly as she quickly walked away. Alan and I continued our conversation. He asked me if I wanted to go to a popular restaurant that offered dozens of decadent desserts. I didn't think about Marsha, not until after Alan had driven me home, taken my phone number, told me how much he had enjoyed spending time with me, and kissed me good night. As my key turned in the lock to the side door, I wondered why all the lights were on in the house. Grandma greeted me at the door. "You're out for hours having a good time, while your sister is in the hospital."

Hours later, Marsha returned with Dad and our neighbor Carl, whom Marsha had a secret crush on. Once again, Carl was there to save the day. Marsha had dislocated her elbow, which now was back in place, but in the process, a doctor had fractured a bone in her arm. She would need surgery. Since Marsha wasn't covered by Dad's insurance, the operation would have to take place at a different hospital, one run by New York City.

A HELLISH DAY

The next day I paid for the perfect evening I had just enjoyed. Our neighbor Rick drove Mom, Dad, and Marsha to the city hospital early in the morning. The surgery was supposed to last an hour, and I was in charge of Ian and Jay. The day was beastly hot, and we didn't have any air-conditioning. At one time, my parents did have an air conditioner in their bedroom—it came with the house. But one day my father decided to clean the window, the one that held the air conditioner in place. What he didn't know—or think about—was that the air conditioner was not held in place with brackets, screws, or any of the usual paraphernalia. As he opened the window, the air conditioner tumbled out, smashing onto the driveway below. While that incident spelled the end of cool summer nights for my parents, we all realized how lucky we were that no one happened to be walking up the driveway as the air conditioner careened downward. Luck was not often on our side, but this time it was.

Almost as soon as Marsha and my parents left for the hospital, Ian became agitated because Mom and Marsha were not around. Ian pulled my hair and pinched my arms. He managed to find the most sensitive spot on the inside part of my upper arm. It hurt like the sting of a very angry bee. Finally, to protect myself, I draped a heavy quilt around myself as I took care of Ian. While sweating, I did what I could to entertain Ian, keep him safe, and prevent major damage to the house. I didn't bother with any of his exercises that day. Jay sang for Ian, but nothing that day was working to calm our brother down. Every once in a while, I removed the heavy quilt that I was using as armor for a few moments of cooling relief. Seeing an opportunity to attack my bare skin, Ian would find me, again and again, and pinch me until I re-wrapped myself in the quilt. I could feel those broken blood vessels emerging and knew I would need to avoid sleeveless tops for a while—I didn't need questions about the origin of those ugly black-and-blue marks on my upper arm.

By late afternoon, I was a nervous wreck, wondering why no one had called with news about Marsha. Finally, at five o'clock, Mom and Dad arrived home with Marsha, her arm wrapped in a cast from her wrist almost to her shoulder. "Why didn't you call? I was so worried," I said. Mom said she was sorry, they hadn't realized how long everything would take. Mainly I was relieved and glad to get out of the quilt and into a shower. Marsha and I had dinner together and then went to our bedroom to talk. She was in great spirits, largely because the anesthesia hadn't worn off, and to some degree because she had been the center of attention for a full day.

     Harriet S. Mosatche

And Carl had come in to see how she was doing. Marsha had a summer school class the next day, and she was determined to take the train into Manhattan to get there. With Mom and Dad trying to get Ian to sleep, Marsha decided she needed to shower and wash her hair. She was not about to appear on the first day of class with oily hair. While reading in bed, I heard a crash from the bathroom. I ran in to see Marsha slumped over in the shower. Passing out, she had hit her head on the water faucet in the shower stall. The day from hell clearly hadn't ended yet. Fortunately, that injury didn't result in another trip to the emergency room, and life went back to normal—or as normal as things could be in our household.

While Marsha was recuperating, she could not participate in the patterning sessions, so the rest of us had to take up the slack. In spite of periodic setbacks, Ian seemed to be improving. He was less destructive and aggressive, piled blocks on top of each other better than I could, and seemed to be trying to speak. I didn't know if what I saw was the result of wishful thinking or actual change, but even small signs kept us sticking to the program. And we kept reading those reports that described dramatic changes in other kids. Ian was going to be one of those successes.

MAKING CRITICAL DECISIONS

By the time I was a college sophomore, I had decided to major in psychology and was no longer interested in becoming a Kindergarten teacher. Psychology, the science of behavior, was a field I could see being very useful in helping others like Ian. I began to use the jargon—reinforcement, stages of development, conditioning. Marsha and I were busy with normal college activities for the late 1960's— studying, dating, spending time with friends, and marching in protests.

Whenever I could, I played Ian's favorite songs on the Sohmer upright piano that Mom had played on as a child. I sang *This Old Man, She'll Be Coming 'Round the Mountain, The Hokey Pokey,* and *Blue Suede Shoes.* Although I didn't know all the words to those songs, and sometimes hit the wrong notes, Ian appreciated my musical skills more than anyone else. But then again, Ian also enjoyed Marsha's totally off-key rendition of *The Impossible Dream*, something that would have been painful to anyone with even a remote sense of pitch. My younger brother Jay was around a lot and Ian loved hearing him sing, but only certain songs. When Ian didn't like a particular melody, he let us know by grunting. When he enjoyed a song, he clasped his hands around the back of his head while smiling broadly or clapped his ears lightly. People who didn't know Ian's manner of expressing delight thought that he was putting his hands over his ears to show his distress. I had to explain that Ian wasn't trying to block out the sounds, that he was actually trying to maximize a pleasant sensation. Although Ian was not able to speak, he understood a great deal and delighted in pointing to an item mentioned in a particular song, even before it was said. His receptive language was so good that he could fill in large parts of Dr. Seuss books, such as touching the top of his head when the line was: "The cat in the (*hat*)" or pointing to his eyes for the phrase, "and to think that I (*saw*) it on Mulberry Street."

Patterning continued to be a part of our lives, but gradually, I realized that the changes we were seeing were probably the result of the extraordinary amount of attention showered on Ian, the almost non-stop stimulation of all his senses and the constant reinforcement of certain behaviors, and not the effect of a real change in his brain. The neighbors continued to be willing to come over for patterning, but they were not as enthusiastic as they had been when they first started. When Mom and Dad told us they were considering stopping the program, we talked about the changes we saw in Ian, but also about how we would have more time for other things. Guilt was part of the picture—each of us questioned whether we should really stop. Marsha strongly voiced her opinion that we continue patterning, that we should we give it a bit more time. But for the rest of us, the bittersweet decision was, "We're done."

CHAPTER 6

Changing Priorities

During my last college year (1969-1970), I divided my time and energy among anti-Vietnam war rallies, classes and tests, friends and dates, and Ian. As he reached puberty and was bigger and stronger, he became even more of a challenge for our family. Marsha and I continued to keep a lock on our bedroom door so Ian would not come in while we were studying. Marsha graduated from college a year before me and had gotten a job at the Metropolitan Life Insurance Company in New York, and typically was only able to care for Ian on the weekends. I had applied to a Masters degree psychology program at Hunter College and knew I would have to make some money during the summer so I could afford the tuition and fees. I hated to lie, but I told the man who would become my boss the summer after graduation that I was hoping to make a career at the insurance company where my sister worked. I guess I sounded convincing when I told him that going to graduate school was not something I had considered, and that I was ready to begin work immediately. I got the job and so did my friend Nancy, who had once again become my best friend after a few years of a break in our relationship during high school. I was a management trainee in the Actuarial Department, even though I had no idea what actuaries did. From the moment I started that job, I began the countdown to the day 11 weeks later when I would be leaving to start grad school. I spent hours looking for mathematical errors, and found them ranging from a penny to a million dollars.

Not that the job was so bad. My boss allowed me the flexibility that Nancy wasn't permitted. While she had to return from lunch exactly 36 minutes after it started, I window-shopped or wandered around the area near the office for an extra ten minutes each day.

MEETING LUC

The weekend before graduate school began, I celebrated the end of 11 weeks in the Actuarial Department by taking the bus to the beach where I could meet guys—a common theme in my young life—and escape from the chaos at home. After a few hours of swimming—or more accurately dog paddling—reading, and walking along the water's edge, I packed up my stuff and began to leave the beach. A French accented "Leaving so soon?" stopped me.

"I've been here for hours," I answered, noticing the blue eyes and thick, blondish-brown wavy hair that accompanied the French accent.

"If you stay for a while longer, I'll drive you home," he said.

I sat down on his blanket, and we began to talk. I had time to decide whether he was an ax murderer or just a cute guy who might be interesting to date while I settled into life as a graduate student. I had just broken up with a summer boyfriend, a rich but shallow guy who had been the perfect seasonal distraction.

Luc, as I found out, had been born in Tunisia and had recently completed a four-year stint with the U.S. Marines. Noticing the American flag decal on his car window, I hesitated before getting in. I told him that I was surprised that his car sported a flag. That was the symbol favored by those who supported the Vietnam war, and, as a political activist against that war, I did not want to get involved with someone whose views would be so different from mine. But the French accent and blue eyes won out, and I took the ride home. Of course, I didn't ask him to come in to meet my family. I hadn't yet told Luc about Ian. That would come later, and only if a conversation on the beach and a ride home turned into something more meaningful.

 Harriet S. Mosatche

Luc removed the flag decal from his car window, and we began to date regularly, soon deciding that we would not date anyone else. I learned that his parents had divorced years ago and that he now lived with his father while his mother lived in France. He learned that I was one of four children with the youngest having severe disabilities. Falling in love was easy—Luc was an escape from the turmoil at home. His father often worked nights, which allowed us quiet, intimate times together at his apartment.

I received a stipend that covered my first year's graduate school tuition, which eased my concern about whether I could pay for required textbooks and subway and bus fare. During the following summer, I became a research assistant for a professor, which meant even more time away from home. Half-way through the summer, Professor Brown asked if I would be willing to spend a few days with her family on Martha's Vineyard, a place I had never heard of. That way we could continue to work on her research project, and I would get a bit of a vacation myself. So this Brooklyn girl packed her bag and went off to the Vineyard. The experience was unlike any I had ever had—a simple request at the dinner table to pass the butter turned into a lengthy philosophical conversation, and a party I attended with the professor and her husband opened my eyes to how writers and professors talked about the issues of the day.

CONTINUING MY EDUCATION

Early in the second year of my Master's program at Hunter College, I learned that my friend Nancy was applying to the social psychology doctoral program at the Graduate Center of the City University of New York. She informed me that without a Ph.D., you really couldn't do anything worthwhile, so I decided to apply, too, but to a different program, one in developmental psychology. My dream continued to be to make life better for children, but I had decided not to pursue clinical psychology. I already had enough drama in my life—I didn't think I could stay detached and helpful when learning firsthand about the tragedies of other people's lives. Better to be a researcher.

As I read the letter accepting me into my first-choice doctoral program, I beamed. But reality quickly took hold—now I had to get through it. Years earlier, I had watched a television program in which a female student fell apart during her oral defense and never received her degree. That nightmare scenario stayed with me for a long time. I continued to live at home during the first six months of my doctoral program, and although I became pretty friendly with the other students, I did not tell them about Ian. The story was just too complicated, and I had learned to compartmentalize my life so that there was school, Luc, my work as a research assistant, and Ian.

A BREAKING POINT

Luc accepted Ian and understood how painful his disability was to me and my family, and how much I continued to hope that life for Ian would get better. Getting a Ph.D. was a way out of the poverty and helplessness that engulfed my parents, so while other students dropped out of the program, took a reduced course load some semesters, or delayed taking their doctoral exams, I adhered to a strict schedule. The lock on the door to the bedroom Marsha and I shared allowed me to study and write papers. Sometimes I heard crashes downstairs, sometimes I heard screaming, but I learned to decipher whether a situation really warranted my intervention. I tried to be available to care for Ian when Mom was at her breaking point and for my nighttime job of putting Ian to sleep. Often, I stayed for hours at Luc and his dad's apartment, where the only things that broke my concentration were the sounds from the kitchen when his dad prepared a gourmet meal for us.

Although I had a part-time research position, I began to look into adjunct teaching positions and applied for one at Brooklyn College. After scheduling a phone interview, I informed Mom that I was going to be on the phone for a while in my room and could not be interrupted. I carefully locked the door and started my phone call. It was going well, when suddenly Ian pushed against the door, forcing the latch open and running into the room. Although upset,

            Harriet S. Mosatche

I figured that my mom would quickly realize that Ian had come upstairs and would take him away. But she didn't. Ian tugged at my hair, while I did my best to keep my voice calm. I guess I could have said, "Excuse me, there's someone at the door" or something like that, but I didn't. I just kept talking, while Ian pulled my hair out by their roots. Tears of pain and frustration welled up in my eyes, but I kept talking. When I finally got off the phone, I screamed at my mother: "How could you let Ian come into my room? Didn't you realize where he was?" I knew my mother felt terrible, but I didn't care. I was furious that I had to live this way. I called Luc and asked him to take me away from there and went outside to wait for him. As we drove around, I talked about my mixed emotions—I felt guilty because I loved Ian so much, but living with him was more than I could handle sometimes. And this was one of those times.

MOVING OUT

While my relationship with Luc was becoming more serious, Marsha started dating Larry. What made Larry particularly special to Marsha was his immediate acceptance of Ian. When Larry came over to pick up Marsha, he would go over to Ian and say, "Hi Tiger. How are you doing?" And Ian reacted with a welcoming smile. He sensed who was afraid of him and who was not. Marsha eventually broke up with Larry, recognizing that kindness toward her brother was not a sufficient basis for a relationship.

Two and a half years after Luc and I met, we were married in a local synagogue. The ceremony was brief, and only about a dozen family members attended. A couple of neighbors cared for Ian while Luc, I, and our guests celebrated at a restaurant near the synagogue. Luc and I found an apartment not far from the beach where we met, one we could afford with our part-time jobs—me as an adjunct psychology instructor and him as a management trainee. I went home to visit Ian and the rest of the family often, but Marsha, still living at home, was the one who spent most of her non-working time taking care of Ian to give Mom and Dad a break.

CHAPTER 7

New Environments for Ian

Soon after Luc and I married, Marsha left her job at the Metropolitan Life Insurance Company and found something closer to home. The position she took at Kings County Hospital as a financial care investigator allowed her to make new friends, but it was one particular co-worker who caught her eye. His name was Steve, and he began to drive her home from work each night. This relationship seemed more serious than others Marsha had been involved in, and I wanted to meet this new guy. I didn't want to seem too obvious, so I lugged my 10-pound developmental psychology handbook out to the driveway of my parents' home where I was visiting and busied myself with highlighting key passages as I awaited the arrival of the green sports car Steve drove. Marsha's face was aglow as she got out of his car—she was in love. Less than 10 months after my own wedding, Marsha and Steve married.

CRUSHING CHALLENGES

Mom and Dad were genuinely delighted that their daughters were married, but everyday life proved to be significantly more difficult for them after we left. Ian's routine had changed, and he often reacted to change with agitation and aggression. Not infrequently, we received phone calls from Mom when caring for Ian overwhelmed her. Luc drove me over—I did not get a drivers' license until I was in my thirties. Or Steve drove Marsha over—she didn't drive either and never learned. Mom hated depending on us so much—she wanted us to live happy, independent lives. Sometimes Mom didn't need to ask us for help or explain what was going on—we heard desperation in her voice. One or both of us got over there as quickly as we could, fearing for Mom's health.

As his teen years marched on, Ian got bigger, stronger, and faster. Finding a day-time care program for him became a critical effort. But the answer was always the same: "We are not set up to provide care for someone who is so disabled." While we were searching for a day or residential facility that would accept Ian, a young reporter named Geraldo Rivera did a televised exposé on the horrific conditions at the Willowbrook State School that finally hit a public nerve. Naked children surrounded by excrement and filth, distraught children banging their heads against walls, frightened children force-fed disgusting mush. I was terrified that Ian would land in a place like that since other options were closed to us.

Ian's pediatrician suggested that we take him to a city hospital and say that Ian is out of control and needs to be evaluated. The doctor told us that after the evaluation, Ian would be placed in a facility. No one wanted to take that step, but Mom couldn't take care of Ian on her own any longer. Ian was considerably taller and stronger than her. So my parents took Ian, at the age of 15, to Kings County Hospital where he was admitted on April 20, 1974. By that time, Dad had gotten a job as a pharmacy aide at that hospital, and he would be able to visit Ian during his lunch break. It sounded like a good plan. We explained to Ian that he would be staying there for a little while and that we would see him soon. It's impossible to know how much Ian understood, but all of us were teary-eyed as we left each other.

Ian was placed in the adolescent psychiatric unit. Other residents there were awaiting evaluation or placement after stabbing a teacher, shooting a parent, or cutting a wrist hoping to die. Ian was the only one who had a severe developmental disability and couldn't speak. After the psychiatrist on duty indicated that he could not do an evaluation due to Ian's agitation, another physician said he would try different dosages of Thorazine and other drugs to calm him. Dad visited Ian every day while Mom sent out letters and made phone calls to possible facilities or agencies that might be able to help. I visited as often as I could, usually with Marsha and Steve, and sometimes with Luc or Mom, Dad, and Jay, and following those visits, I described Ian's condition in a diary. While initially Ian seemed to be fairly alert and responsive, he quickly began to show side effects of the medications he was on. Sitting restrained in a wheelchair, his hands and feet shook. He was unable to keep his head up. Five days after Ian was admitted to the hospital, his drug dosage was reduced, he seemed more alert, and Marsha and Dad were given permission to take Ian off the unit briefly so he could run around the corridor.

That was the end of the good news. Things went downhill quickly. A week after Ian's admission to the hospital, Dad found Ian tied to his bed wearing "mittens" because he was "hitting himself," Dad was told. I visited Ian the next day. I needed to tell him that we loved him, and that he wouldn't have to stay there for long. I met Dad at the unit, and we entered the crowded main room. I wasn't prepared for what I saw. Ian, in a straitjacket, wore a look of terror along with a black eye and a couple of other facial bruises. Tears welled up in my eyes as I bent over to kiss him. I found a nurse and asked how Ian got the injuries and why he was being restrained. "It's for his own protection," she said. "We have some very violent residents here, and if Ian touches them, they attack him."

"Can't you find some other way to protect him? Ian doesn't understand why he's in a straitjacket. He can't speak so the only way he can make his wishes known is by using his hands." The nurse listened sympathetically to my concerns, but said the hospital was following standard practice. "How long will the evaluation take?" I inquired. She didn't have any answers. I kissed Ian again before the nurse led me out—visiting time was over. Dad and I talked briefly

        Harriet S. Mosatche

in the hall—he had to go back to work. While on the bus back to my parents' house, I worked hard to keep my emotions in check. As my mom opened the door for me, the tears came along with deep, heaving sobs. "We have to get him out of there," I finally managed to say. "It's worse than anything I've ever seen."

AGAINST DOCTORS' ORDERS

When Marsha and her husband Steve visited Ian a couple of days later, an aide told them there were too many other visitors and they couldn't see him then. They suspected that wasn't the real story. Knowing their way around the hospital, they found an administrator who allowed them to visit. Ian's face was swollen and bruised.

Weeks went by without progress in getting Ian into a school or residential facility or finding the appropriate drug regimen to control his behavior. My parents contacted the doctors in charge of Ian's care but couldn't get much information about what was being done either in terms of evaluation or a treatment plan. Ian's meds were increased, but he was still restrained. Along with bruises on his face and legs, the skin on his hands had begun to peel. Ian's doctors said they needed more time. For what, I wondered.

Steve asked his brother's friend, a lawyer, to represent us in trying to get the evaluation completed and Ian out of the hospital and into a better facility. He asked us to take Polaroid photos to demonstrate the abuse Ian was suffering. When staff noticed Steve taking photos, they tried to get the camera out of his hands, but Steve and Marsha managed to run out of the ward with their camera intact. I attended the meeting arranged by the lawyer at which the doctor and administrator kept repeating that Ian was not ready to be released, but they could not provide any information about what would be done for him if he were to be kept there longer. Kings County was a dead end, and we needed to get Ian out of there before even worse damage was done. My parents signed the "against doctor's orders" release form, and we took Ian home with us.

That night, Ian kept kissing us, letting us know how relieved and happy he was to be home, but his affection made us feel guilty that we had allowed him to be restrained for so long. We knew we still needed a longer-term solution, but having Ian home and out of the tight restraining device was good enough for the moment.

Harriet S. Mosatche

CHAPTER 8

My Letter-Writing Campaign Followed by Some Success

n between classes, studying, and working as an adjunct instructor at Hunter College, I made calls or wrote letters about Ian. Maybe if I were eloquent and passionate enough, I could convince someone in government how critical it was to find a day school or residential facility for Ian. I was the self-appointed spokesperson and advocate in our family for Ian. In one of my stuffed file cabinets in the basement are letters from Senator Edward Kennedy, Representative Hugh Carey (who later became governor of New York), and a bunch of other politicians or their assistants, all of whom responded to my written pleas for help with finding placement for Ian. Not that those letters resulted in any concrete assistance, but they offered sympathy and some suggestions, none of which led to any solutions. Dad even called John J. O'Connor, at that time the television critic for The New York Times, who had been a regular customer at the deli where Dad had worked in the 1960's and early 1970's. Maybe a press connection could help. Although O'Connor was sympathetic, he said he couldn't think of anything he could do.

A MOVE INTO THE BROOKLYN DEVELOPMENTAL CENTER

It was U.S. Congressional Representative Elizabeth Holtzman from New York, better known to most Baby Boomers as a member of the Watergate panel, who provided tangible support by having one of her aides work with us to get Ian into the Brooklyn Developmental Center (BDC). Those were the days of large institutions, typically located in places where no one else wanted to live. BDC was built on swampland in Brooklyn. It had a large one-story building and several two-story residential buildings. When my family visited, before deciding to move Ian to BDC, the facility seemed clean and safe. Some residents walked around by themselves and greeted us. The residential areas or "wings" didn't seem very cheerful, but at least some of the caregivers interacted with the residents. Six months had elapsed since Ian's miserable "evaluation" experience at Kings County. Ian's new residence has to be better than that, I thought, as my parents and I left Ian in BDC's infirmary on an early October day in 1974. The infirmary was where Ian would be evaluated before being placed in one of the residential areas. Although he was chronologically 15, he was still a helpless child. Tears streamed down my face as I walked away

Mom and Dad visited Ian a few times that first week, and reported back that Ian seemed to be clean and well fed, although he was still in the infirmary pending a move to a residential wing with activities. It will get better, I told myself. I had seen places for Ian to run at BDC and even a pool for him to enjoy. Luc, Marsha, and I visited on the weekend, and I was upset that Ian was still in the infirmary and getting minimal custodial care. Although I understood that staff would not love him the way we had, I had hoped staff would talk to him and show him some affection.

After a few weeks, Ian was transferred to the second floor of one of the residential buildings. He shared a room with Bill, a slim boy with a welcoming smile who uttered a few words occasionally. I saw Ian's move into the wing as a good sign—the next step would be for Ian to start participating in a program that would teach him skills and allow him some measure of happiness. Ian smiled and clapped his ears when I visited, and he held onto me to keep me from leaving when I started putting on my jacket. I always left reluctantly to go back to the rest of my life—school, work, and a husband.

　　Harriet S. Mosatche

AN ALARMING PHONE CALL

Just as Mom and Dad were getting into some kind of normal routine, and I was paying more attention to my schoolwork, a phone call on November 10, 1974 changed everything. Dad called from Brookdale Hospital in Brooklyn (the hospital where Ian, Jay, Marsha, and I had been born) to say that Ian had been badly beaten; I needed to get there right away. Luc dropped me off at the hospital entrance, and with my heart beating so fast and so loud that I thought it would explode out of my chest, I frantically searched for the Emergency Room. Someone with a swollen bloody face was in a bed, but I couldn't tell who it was until I saw Dad and knew that bruised face had to be Ian's. How could this have happened? Every part of his body was bruised, but it was that unrecognizable face that shook me violently. Ian had suffered a head trauma from the beating. His arms and legs were totally discolored; he had bite marks on his chest and stomach; a nerve injury paralyzed one hand and nails had been torn from two fingers.

Initially, the doctors accused my parents of brutally beating Ian, but quickly they learned that Ian had been brought to the hospital from an institution. Because Ian was not verbal, I would never learn about the emotional impact of the attack, but I was sure the effects would be long-lasting, maybe even permanent. It was not easy discovering the truth, but the story that emerged was that Ian's roommate Bill had beaten Ian during the night and when the early morning shift arrived, they found my brother bloodied and barely conscious. Upset as I was, I did not blame Bill for the attack. After all, he, too, was a resident. But where were the staff members who were responsible for keeping Ian safe? While Ian couldn't fight back, he must have made some noise while being pummeled and bitten by Bill. The injuries were so extensive that it had to have taken a long time to inflict them. I've imagined those horrific moments many times over the years.

During Ian's stay in the hospital, his only visitors were his immediate family. Most of our relatives did not have a relationship with

Ian, but some did call to get updates on his condition. Gradually, Ian's physical bruises healed enough for him to leave the hospital and return to the BDC infirmary where he continued his recovery and received physical therapy once in a while. Ian returned to his wing, and, amazingly, our family had to fight to prevent him from being placed back in the room he had shared with Bill. Administrators promised that the procedures had changed, that supervision was better now. As trusting as my parents typically were, they had learned in the most painful way to be a bit more skeptical, and said they wanted Ian placed with a different roommate, someone who did not have a history of violence and who had a calmer temperament. However, Bill stayed in Ian's wing, and Ian continued to be the target of his anger. During the winter of 1974 to 1975, Ian received stitches to his nose, toe, and head and suffered several black eyes inflicted by Bill. So much for better supervision. As horrible as the situation continued to be, we had not found an alternative day or residential program. And moving Ian back home was just not a realistic option.

BORED, RESTRAINED, AND DRUGGED

Ian was often heavily drugged and appeared too lethargic and disoriented to enjoy our visits or to defend himself from attack. Even when his drug dosage seemed more reasonable, Ian basically had nothing to do. He often sat in a "geriatric chair" from which he could not get up, making him an easy target. At times he was restrained with what BDC staff called a camisole, but was little more than an abbreviated straitjacket. In time, Ian became self-abusive, something he had never done while he was home. He bit his arms and scratched at scabs on his legs. When I explained to BDC staff that Ian was doing those things because he had nothing better to do, that he was bored by the total lack of stimulation, I was looked at as if I, too, had a disability and was talking gibberish. During one visit to BDC, we found Ian alone in his room tied to a chair that had toppled over.

 Harriet S. Mosatche

My parents and Jay visited a couple of times a week, taking car service because there was no available public transportation to this isolated place. They brought food they knew Ian loved and shared stories and songs with him. On the weekend, Luc and I visited, and sometimes, Marsha and Steve did, too. I hated to leave Ian at the end of our visit, and it took several hours to get out of the despair that engulfed me. I had learned to compartmentalize my life years earlier—Ian existed in one sphere and the rest of my life inhabited a totally separate domain. When Ian's condition was particularly poor, it was hard to transport myself from one compartment to the other, but I certainly tried.

In the summer of 1975, Luc and I planned a trip to Europe. I had never been on a plane, and my first time was to be a transatlantic flight. We were only planning to be away for a couple of weeks, but I was concerned about how Ian would handle my absence. I was afraid that he would feel abandoned, as if I were never returning, even though I had told him about the trip and assured him that I would be back. My dissertation adviser was spending his sabbatical year in London, so that city was our first stop. Then we went on to Paris, where Luc's mother lived. My French was not great since I had not taken advantage of what could have been a live-in French tutor. But I knew how to ask where the bathrooms were located and how to identify that a store was having a sale.

As soon as I returned to New York, I went to BDC and Ian greeted me with the broadest smile, quiet kisses, and lots of ear clapping. I told him about flying on planes just like the ones we saw when Luc occasionally drove him to Kennedy airport. While the trip to Europe had been fun and romantic, real life waited for me back in Brooklyn.

ADVOCATING FOR BETTER TREATMENT

Appalled by the lack of action to provide Ian with a more humane and less dreary existence, my parents did the best job they could at badgering administrators—by phone and in person—for some kind of program for him. I wrote letters for my mother to sign, laying out the dismal situation Ian was in and recommending some reasonable remedial actions. Why was it so difficult to put together a program for Ian? Didn't it make more sense to have Ian participate in music or physical activities instead of having him tear at his skin for stimulation? When months went by with promises but no follow-through, my parents sought the help of my cousin's husband, a lawyer. Marty wrote on his firm's letterhead to the executive director of BDC, advising him that Ian's family had retained him as their attorney and requesting a meeting to discuss "the status of Ian's developmental and custodial care." I prepared a chronology of Ian's experiences at BDC along with program suggestions and sat in at the meeting that Marty arranged. Soon after that meeting, Bill was finally moved to a different residential wing and Ian was given a minimal program of half-hour occupational therapy sessions every weekday morning and afternoon. Not enough, but a small victory for Ian.

After learning in 1975 about the existence of an advocacy group formed by parents of BDC residents called the Spring Creek Association for Retarded Children, I joined. Although I was the only sibling member, I played an active role and became the co-chair of the education committee. I recognized that being a doctoral student might carry some weight. Although I cared about what happened to all the residents at the facility, mainly I was hoping that my advocacy would benefit Ian. Dr. L was the chairperson of the committee and a member of the Brooklyn College faculty. He had a child who was a resident at BDC. Dr L and I conducted in-depth interviews with eight senior members of the BDC administration, including the principal psychologist, the education director, and the director of employee education and training, and we observed programs in action. Then we prepared a three-page report of key findings, which we shared with the full association and with the administration. In part, we wrote that there "is a wall of separation" between Program (education and therapy) and Wings (where the residents live).

     Harriet S. Mosatche

Both of us, as professional educators, are appalled by this situation. Staff in Wing and Program should be in constant contact. What residents learn in Program should be reinforced daily in the Wings. Program personnel should have the opportunity to work with the residents on the Wings and to train Wing personnel. Wing staff should be intimately involved in the planning and carrying out of educational and training programs both on and off the residential Wings... The institution should be entirely reorganized to more fully carry out the Service Plans.

Frustratingly, no one seemed interested in creating an "interdisciplinary team approach," the strategy that Dr. L and I were advocating, and after a while, I dropped out of the Spring Creek Association.

In 1975, the Education for All Handicapped Children Act, PL94-142, became law in the United States and required that children with disabilities not be excluded from public schools because of their disabilities. In addition, school districts were required to provide special services to meet the needs of all children registered there and to teach "handicapped" children in a setting that was as similar as possible to the regular school program. That same year, the Developmentally Disabled Assistance and Bill of Rights Act, providing protection and advocacy services, became the law in this country. Unfortunately, the changes in law didn't seem to change the way Ian was treated.

CHAPTER 9

Ups and Downs of Life at BDC

Each family member developed special routines for entertaining Ian, those things we knew would make him laugh and clap his hands over his ears with delight. Jay had special songs, which allowed Ian to fill in words by pointing to a body part such as his chest to indicate "heart" or leg to show the word "walk." Ian never tired of hearing these songs. Mom was mainly in charge of nourishment, appropriate for a good Jewish mother. Once Ian was moved to BDC, Mom had started cooking and baking special treats for Ian. It was good for her to have something concrete she could do to bring him pleasure. Dad recited stories that he knew would make Ian laugh. And Marsha and I did our own unique routines based on school experiences or television commercials, wherever we could find humorous material.

STORIES BASED ON REAL LIFE

Dad created one particular favorite routine that was eventually taken over by others when Dad became too ill to recite it. This was Dad's version, said with a thick nasal accent:

When I was six years old I went to school. My first grade teacher said to me: "What's your name?"

I said: "My name is Willie Dreshen."

     Harriet S. Mosatche

The teacher asked: "What?"

I said: "My name is Willie Dreshen."

Again, the teacher said: "What?"

My name is Willie Dreshen. Can't you understand English? (My dad used an exaggerated air of frustration for this line.)

My teacher said: "I can't understand you. I think you need an operation."

So I had an operation, but I still talked like this.

On the first day of second grade, my teacher asked me: "What's your name?"

I said: "Willie Dreshen."

The teacher said: "What?"

I answered: "Willie Dreshen. Can't you understand English?"

The teacher said: "I think you need an operation."

So I had an operation but I still talked like this.

The story continued through a number of grades with Willie having a corresponding number of operations. Ian often said "What" (or at least a hoarse Wa sound) at the appropriate time. The long part of the story had Willie Dreshen finishing high school, and that's where the story stopped being repetitious.

I went to the senior prom and there I saw a beautiful girl.

"Do you want to dance?" I asked her.

"Why don't you blow your nose?" she responded.

So I blew my nose and now I talk like this. (At that point, my father stopped using a nasal voice.)

When Ian listened to this story, he gleefully clapped his hands over his ears and grinned. I think he liked the repetition, the pretend nasal voice, and the name Willie Dreshen. Years after my father started telling the story, I found out that Willie Dreshen was a real person, one of my father's classmates. The operations didn't happen or at least not in the repetitive way expressed in the story. Nor did blowing his nose cure Willie Dreshen. Because of Ian's delight with this story, Willie Dreshen became a beloved person in our family.

Aside from Willie Dreshen who was only famous in our family, Dad regaled the rest of the family with stories about other people who were part of his formative years and became famous or infamous in the larger world. Julius Rosenberg lived in my father's neighborhood and the two boys played together. Part of their bond might have been due to the fact that they shared a surname. But my father always insisted that Julius Rosenberg was not guilty of conspiracy to commit espionage, the crime for which he and his wife Ethel were executed in 1953. Then there was my father's classmate Leon Klinghoffer, who unintentionally became famous when he was thrown overboard by terrorists in 1985 on the *Achille Lauro* cruise ship. Neither the Julius Rosenberg story nor the Leon Klinghoffer incident ever became routines for Ian—they were both just too tragic.

It took a lot of trial and error to find out which stories made Ian laugh and which made him grunt—his way of saying "Stop—this is boring." One story that did make the cut, even becoming one of Ian's favorites, was based on my experience in ninth grade when my beloved algebra teacher was transferred mid-year to a different school and replaced by a couple of substitutes. Here is one version of that story as we told it to Ian:

When I was in ninth grade, the phone rang at home. It was Mr. Cohen. "I'm being transferred to another school. I need your help. Please send a telegram to Albany."

　　　　Harriet S. Mosatche

We didn't have the money for a telegram, so we sent a letter to Albany (where the state board of education was located). By the time the letter got to Albany, it was TOO LATE, and Mr. Cohen was TRANSFERRED. (The important words were exaggerated, and anyone in the room when the story was recited was expected to say the words at the same time—like a chorus.)

The next day, a new teacher, Mr. Schmendrick (not his real name but one that fit his demeanor), showed up, (At that point in the story, I would play the part of Mr. Schmendrick walking awkwardly and slowly into the classroom.)

"How much is two plus two?"(I asked in a timid tone as I faced a pretend blackboard while writing imaginary numbers on it.)

"Very good, very good." (Instead of answering the question, a family member spoke up in a high-pitched childish voice portraying my classmates and me.)

"How much is three plus three?" (I asked playing Mr. Schmendrick to the hilt.)

"Very good, very good." (spoken by "students" aka family members)

"Why are you doing this to me? I am just trying to teach you algebra. I will give you one more chance. How much is four plus four?" (said in a very whiny voice)

"Very good. Very good."

(At that point, "Mr. Schmendrik" walks dejectedly out of the room.)

The next day, a new teacher came to class. His name was Mr. Grossman and he was very strict. He called me over and said: "Harriet, you have to tutor Jill. If she fails, you fail."

"Jill, you have to study algebra."

"No, I'm not interested in algebra," (Jill said in a raised voice with me playing all the parts). "I am only interested in Communism. You should be studying the Communist Manifesto."

(I act out a struggle between Jill and me.)

"To my great relief, Jill passed algebra."

While Ian did not understand complex concepts, such as communism and algebra, he loved the sound of the words, the different accents and tones we took on in telling the stories, the acting out of the scenes, and the repetition. He never grew tired of the Mr. Schmendrick story. There really was a girl in my ninth grade class who was a poor Algebra student and actually tried to convince her classmates that Communism was a shining example of a political system. I often wonder how her life turned out. In any event, her antics in ninth grade provided me with a story that Ian enjoyed.

ILLNESS AND MORE INJURIES

During the winter of 1976, when Ian was 17, he developed a severe case of hepatitis. He had been ill for several weeks before he was hospitalized with diarrhea, loss of weight, and skin lesions. Although my family repeatedly called the staff's attention to these symptoms, Ian was not brought to the hospital for testing until he became jaundiced. After a brief hospitalization, he was brought back to the BDC infirmary, where he was kept isolated and in some kind of restraints for two months. During this long period of recuperation, Ian was not given any kind of physical therapy, and by the time he left the infirmary, his gait was unsteady and his coordination poor. Soon after returning to his residential wing, Ian began to have epileptic seizures. Initially, the facility's doctor claimed that these were not real seizures, that he believed that Ian was merely imitating other residents. How ironic that the same doctor who treated Ian as if he knew nothing, now believed that Ian had the ability to mimic an elaborate set of behaviors resembling a *grand mal* seizure.

After a brief stay at Brookdale Hospital, Ian returned to the infirmary to rest. I learned that experiencing a *grand mal* seizure is exhausting. Resting was not really possible at BDC—a few days later, Ian was back in the hospital for a deep gash on his head that required stitches, the result of an object thrown by another resident. When I wasn't visiting Ian, I spent a lot of time worrying about him—anticipating another phone call informing me of another "accident."

Ian began to receive medication to try to control his seizures, but injuries and medical issues continued. In early summer of 1976, Ian returned to Brookdale for treatment of a severe fungal infection of his feet, a condition that had been left untreated for weeks, even though my family had repeatedly urged the BDC doctor and administrators to seek medical attention for his feet, which had become red, scaly, itchy, and bloodied. While Ian was in the hospital, he was given Dilantin, which eventually reduced the frequency of seizures.

Three months—August through October—went by without a hospitalization. I no longer jumped when the phone rang, expecting more bad news. However, when I visited Ian around Thanksgiving, I saw that his arm was bandaged so tightly around what I learned was a deep cut that his arm had turned blue. I waited in the wing corridor while Ian was brought to the treatment room where his finger got caught in a stretcher, requiring stitches to close the new gaping wound.

A couple of days later, when Mom and Jay visited, they noticed that Ian's knee was swollen. Soon the swelling extended from Ian's foot all the way to his thigh, which is what my parents saw when they visited just a few days after Mom had first noticed the swelling. They immediately told staff about Ian's condition. I and other family members continued to report to staff what we observed each time we visited over the next couple of weeks. Since this all occurred years before people could look up symptoms on the internet, we had no way to know how serious the swelling was. We relied on the doctors at BDC to recognize and deal with a potentially dangerous condition. Two weeks later, Ian was taken to Brookdale Hospital and put on intravenous antibiotics for cellulitis, a potentially life-threatening infection. After his release, he remained on antibiotics for another month and was scheduled for a follow-up hospital clinic visit in January. That never took place because a male aide to accompany him to the hospital was not available. Today there are patient ombudsmen in hospitals and other resources to contact when a family member believes mistreatment or neglect has occurred. But in the late 1970's there was little recourse aside from nagging. And my family and I had become experts in that behavior. A December 1976 Case Summary report was prepared by a BDC staff supervisor for the facility's director after our family's lawyer (cousin Marty) had again formally requested better treatment of Ian. The medical section of the report included the following:

> *Ian Rosenberg is a 17 year old white male who is functioning within the profound level of retardation. He is hyperactive, abusive to himself and others, and has a history of seizure disorder. In the past few months, Ian has lost several pounds. Dr. W attributes this weight loss to Ian's hyperactive behavior. Ian's weight has remained stable at 86 pounds since last month, however.*
>
> *For the past ten days, Ian has been suffering from the swelling of his right knee and leg. At first, antibiotics were administered but had no effect. Today, therefore, Ian was re-examined by Dr. W and Dr. C. After consultation with Dr. A, the decision was made to send Ian to the surgical clinic at Brookdale Hospital...Ian is scheduled for admission to Brookdale at 12:30 PM today.*

     Harriet S. Mosatche

> *Ian suffers periodically from bruises on various parts of his body. According to Dr. W, these bruises are part of the result of Ian's self-abuse.*

Dr. W was trying hard to protect an institution that was not protecting Ian since some of the bruises were on Ian's back in places he couldn't reach. Moreover, our family had repeatedly mentioned to staff that Ian seemed to be losing weight. The second part of the report to BDC's director focused on occupational therapy. In part, the report read:

> *As of August of this year, Ian had made tremendous progress. His attention span increased to the point where the two half-hour sessions could be replaced by a daily one-hour session, with Ian showing the ability to concentrate on any given task for approximately ten minutes. His interfering behaviors had been eliminated and his abusive behaviors had decreased to such an extent that he had no scars at all on his body and he could go through an entire session without pinching the therapist. At one point he was exposed to a classroom situation and worked on a task in competition with other residents. Ian's dislike of being touched had lessened and he had begun to laugh appropriately and to behave in a playful manner toward the therapist.*
>
> *According to Mr. T, Ian had what appeared to be a seizure in the beginning of November, and he credits this with Ian's current regression. However, Dr. W does not recall a seizure taking place at that time, nor do the medical records have any entry related to it. Mr. T maintains that at the time, Ms. S, also of O.T., went to Brookdale to speak to the doctors about the seizure, but was not able to arrange for them to examine Ian since on a previous occasion they had been unable to examine him due to his behavior.*

ANOTHER BEATING

One wintry night in 1977, history repeated itself with Ian once again a victim of a severe beating. This time it was Edward who entered Ian's bedroom during the night and beat him to the point that Ian was barely recognizable at the hospital: both eyes discolored and swollen with one eye completely closed; his left ear distended; abrasions and contusions on both legs, feet, shoulders, elbows and his right hip; and his neck covered with deep scratches. How could this happen again? I was furious that BDC was so lax in its supervision that my brother was viciously beaten just two years after he had suffered a brutal attack by Bill. I couldn't stand to imagine what Ian was feeling as his head was bashed, his face punched, and the rest of his body deeply scratched by sharp fingernails. Ian was released from the hospital in a few days, but he was back in less than a week, this time with a fever of 105 degrees and a diagnosis of pneumonia. Back in the BDC infirmary several days later, Ian was heavily sedated. I saw that he had fresh bruises on his face. "He must have done it to himself," an aide told us. I heard that excuse many times during Ian's years at BDC, even when the bruises were to a part of the body he could not reach. Since Ian was not verbal, he couldn't tell us what had really happened. The stay in the BDC infirmary didn't last long—Ian was back in the hospital, this time at Kingsbrook, for x-rays of a very swollen foot and ankle and a large bump on the right side of his forehead. No one could explain the source of those injuries.

 Harriet S. Mosatche

February 1977 had started with Edward beating Ian and ended with Edward punching my other brother Jay in the back of the neck. Ian was clearly the intended target, but Jay got in front of Ian just as Edward entered the room, and it was Jay who took the punch, sparing Ian from further injury at least on that date. Unfortunately, family members weren't around most of the time, and Ian continued to suffer. Two days after Jay was punched, Ian was admitted to the ICU of Brookdale Hospital at 3 AM. The doctor revealed that Ian was suffering from dehydration, elevated fever, and contusions and lacerations of his shoulder, legs, and arms. A few teeth were loose and his head was swollen and his face discolored. Internal head trauma was also suspected. Although I tried hard to control my emotions, tears rolled down my cheeks when I saw Ian. I apologized to Ian for everything he had endured and told him how much I loved him and that I was trying to protect him, although not successfully. However much we tried, we still couldn't find a more suitable place for Ian to live. I knew that Ian could not return to my parents' home as they were becoming increasingly frail, and he might well inadvertently hurt them. And if I were to give up my career to try to care for Ian in my small apartment, I recognized that I couldn't do that without help and our family couldn't afford to pay for home health aides. Bringing Ian into my home would also have placed a major, possibly even fatal, strain on my marriage. Feasible alternatives were just not available in the 1970s for a family without huge financial resources.

"How much can one person endure?" I often thought after Ian suffered another large bruise or a debilitating illness. Unfortunately, the answer turned out to be much more than I could have imagined. On March 7, 1977, Ian was again hospitalized, this time because he appeared very weak, not surprising since his weight by this time had decreased to 72 pounds. Ian was 18 years old and 5'6." Although the head doctor at BDC gave us permission to feed Ian whenever we visited, the aides harassed us repeatedly about the food we brought. We knew what Ian liked and we didn't rush him through a meal the way we had seen staff do. Ian almost always appeared to be hungry or thirsty when any of us visited him, constantly pointing to his mouth. He was very clear about his food preferences, and if an item was something he didn't like, he would grimace and spit it out.

INSTITUTIONAL CRUELTY

Sometimes when Ian pointed to his mouth, he was telling us he was in pain. I could distinguish "I want food" or "I want a drink" from "My mouth hurts" since Ian made an unpleasant grunting noise to indicate discomfort. For three months, Ian paired pointing to his mouth with a grunt. I and other members of my family repeatedly asked that Ian be taken to the dentist to check out the source of the pain. "The dentist is ill" so Ian will have to wait, we were told, as if that dentist was the one and only person with a dental degree. Finally, Ian was seen by a dentist who found and filled three large cavities. During those months, not only was Ian dealing with dental discomfort, but he had also developed a severe limp and poor coordination along with a serious eye infection and multiple seizures. My parents, siblings, and I noted large bumps on his forehead, deep lacerations, bruises on his nose, back and eyes, with new injuries showing up on a weekly basis. I tried to prepare myself psychologically for what I might find when I visited BDC. Would Ian be so heavily sedated that he could barely focus or even sit up? What new injuries will have appeared on his body? Will he be wet and soiled? Will he be tied to a chair or restrained in some other fashion?

Periodically, after weeks or months of begging, nagging, and threatening, BDC would schedule a meeting. These were full of hope. My notes from a meeting on March 25, 1977 indicated that Ian would receive further dental treatment at the Mental Retardation Institute in Valhalla and that he would begin toilet training on his wing. Ian was scheduled to begin twice daily 45-minute "educational therapy" sessions. Wing staff members were asked to assist Ian in learning how to use feeding utensils, and the staff

       Harriet S. Mosatche

psychologist was going to help Ian follow commands for an hour a week. I knew that Ian could already do those things—at least when he wanted to—but for Ian to spend time with a psychologist sounded a lot better than being tied to a chair on the wing facing away from a television set blaring with noise from a show that interested staff and certainly not Ian. The plan also included recreational therapy sessions on Monday, Tuesday, and Thursday from 3:00 to 3:30 PM, which might increase Ian's gross motor skills and even more important provide another opportunity to get away from the monotony of his wing. The possibility of art therapy was also mentioned during this meeting. I described the side effects of the drugs (Thorazine, Phenobarbitol, and Dilantin) Ian was on, and the doctor promised to look into modifying the dosages.

If only all this were actually implemented. Here and there were attempts at toilet training, recreational therapy, and teaching Ian to use a fork and a spoon. An hour session became 45 minutes, which was further reduced over time. Three times a week became twice a week, and more often just once. No one was accountable for making sure that these service plans were carried out. Ian's medication dosages were not altered. Staff found it easier to keep him drugged than try to modify his behavior in other ways.

Along with the formal Treatment of Team Review provided to our family was a document from the New York State Department of Mental Hygiene of the Division of Mental Retardation dated March 23, 1977. The subject was the "right to appeal a client's development plan" and laid out all the steps a family could take, ranging from making an informal objection to the Team Leader to making a "further appeal to the Department's Regional Director." By the time three or four steps of the appeal process were completed, families would typically be so disheartened that few would continue on. Besides, it would most likely be time for the next quarterly report, and then they would have to start from step one.

The filling of Ian's cavities precipitated the beginning of his next health challenge. Soon after that dental visit, staff and family noticed that Ian's face was a bit swollen. The swelling increased dramatically over the next few days until it could not be ignored. By April 11, Ian was back at the Mental Retardation Institute at Valhalla with a severe abscess in his mouth and a high fever. One of Ian's eyes was closed. When our family visited the Valhalla facility, we found Ian in a cage, literally a covered cage, like the ones that housed animals in an old zoo. Today, people seeing those conditions would contact the news media, share photos online to get action, send out a Twitter post, maybe even call the police. But in 1977, there were fewer media outlets, the Internet had not yet come into existence, and the public was either unaware of or didn't seem outraged by the inhumane treatment of those with cognitive impairments. Everything was kept under wraps, out of sight.

When I saw Ian in that cage, my guts boiled with anger while tears flooded my eyes. I controlled my emotions since the last thing I wanted was for Ian to see how distressed I was. My job was to cheer Ian up, to show him how much he was loved. While at the Valhalla Institute, Ian suffered new seizures and wasn't released until May 11. While conditions were far from ideal at BDC, at least Ian had a bed there, not a cage.

TRYING TO KEEP IT TOGETHER

Throughout that year, I was teaching a full load of psychology classes at Hunter College, working on my dissertation, and trying to keep my marriage together. What I liked most about teaching was that it required my full focus. When I was explaining Piaget's theory of object permanence or discussing Freud's system of personality, I could not think about Ian's inability to protect himself or about my marital problems. Luc and I had begun to realize how little we had in common, although I was grateful that he continued to visit Ian and take him for car rides. Ian and I sat in the back seat and Ian never tired of hearing and watching me pretend to use a car phone. I don't think such gadgets were available then, but even if they were, they certainly wouldn't be found in the clunker

    Harriet S. Mosatche

that was our car. Sometimes we drove out to Kennedy airport in Queens and as we got closer, Ian began to imitate the sound of a jet engine. Luc was a decent man with a romantic streak that was hard to resist—the delicious dinners, the unexpected flowers, the extravagant gifts (which we couldn't afford), and it was hard to imagine getting divorced. But it was also hard to imagine staying married for the long run and having children with this man. Let's try to work it out, we both said repeatedly. We continued to try as I put my energy into collecting data for my dissertation research.

Two days after Ian returned to BDC, I gave the oral defense for my dissertation. Although I had been teaching at Hunter College for six years, I was still a graduate student, and I was ready, more than ready, to give up that role. I understood that a Ph.D. after my name would open doors, not just in terms of my career but also when I advocated for Ian. Families of those with cognitive disabilities are often treated as if they are also impaired. It would be more difficult to ignore or dismiss me when I introduced myself as Dr. Mosatche. I was overjoyed when my thesis adviser and committee members signed their approval and called me Doctor for the first time. A day later, an entry in the diary I kept about Ian indicated that he had new scratches on his neck.

CHAPTER 10

Promises and Changes

As Ian's condition continued to deteriorate, our family sought help once again from Marty, our lawyer, since it had become clear that threatened legal action and negative publicity were the most effective ways to effect change. Marty had some connections with public officials and managed to arrange a meeting on May 31, 1977 with the New York State Assistant Commissioner of the Department of Mental Hygiene. I brought my detailed notes with me to the meeting along with my suggestions for a program for Ian. Within a week of that meeting, a comprehensive plan had been developed by BDC staff, which included:

1. One-hour sessions five times a week with a psychologist with the "primary emphasis on reducing Ian's aggressive behavior"
2. Two 45-minute daily sessions on weekdays with an occupational therapist to reduce aggressive behavior and increase "educational task performance"
3. Half-hour sessions five days a week "with an assistant teacher on the wing to provide experience with educational material and socialization skills"
4. Three one-half hour sessions weekly "with a recreation therapist on a one to one basis to provide Ian with the opportunity for recreational activities off the wing"

      Harriet S. Mosatche

5. Half-hour sessions five days a week "on a one to one basis with a therapy aide for toilet training and training in activities in daily living"
6. One to one attention seven days a week "from a therapy aide at each meal to provide consistent training in feeding."

The plan was thorough and appropriate, and the letter indicated that it would be in effect upon Ian's return from the Mental Retardation Institute. And yet, in spite of persistent and forceful follow-up from my family and our attorney, the plan was never implemented nor were the "systems for closely monitoring and evaluating progress."

TIME FOR CHANGES

Teaching continued to provide a respite from thoughts of the myriad hardships of Ian's life at BDC as well as from the distressing state of my marriage. After receiving an appointment as an assistant professor for the 1977-1978 academic year at Hunter College, a colleague told me about an opening in the psychology department at the College of Mount St. Vincent in the Bronx borough of New York City. A senior faculty member at Hunter had also advised me to consider moving on. Not because I wasn't doing a great job, she was quick to point out, but because I would continue to be seen as a junior faculty member, someone who had been a student in the department not so long ago. What harm could it do to investigate? And so I applied for the new position. I was still torn about leaving my crumbling marriage, but if I did, starting fresh in a new place was a plus. When the offer was made, I accepted. Luc and I kept trying to keep our marriage together and planned a trip to Barbados in August. By the second day of our vacation, I knew I wanted a trial separation and was ready to start a new life.

Although visiting Ian would be more difficult, I moved out of the Brooklyn apartment I had shared with Luc and into a studio apartment in the Bronx, close to my new job. Dad worried about my living alone, but Mom admired my independence, particularly since her agoraphobia barely allowed her to walk by herself to the corner grocery store. She never visited Ian on her own. I sublet a furnished studio apartment that was affordable but oddly decorated in pineapple style—pineapples on lamps, pillows, and paintings. I was determined to visit Ian every other weekend, even though the trip would take about three hours each way—combining walking, an express bus, a subway, a local bus, and finally car service to a part of Brooklyn that was not served by public transportation. Getting home that same day wasn't feasible, so I made a weekend out of my visit—leaving very early on Saturday morning, visiting Ian, staying with my parents, and then making the return trek on Sunday. I kept to that schedule religiously, no matter what was going on in my life.

Luc and I decided not to make a clean break—neither of us was ready for that. We continued to talk and even see each other once in a while, thinking we might even reconcile. But recognizing our basic incompatibility, I called a divorce lawyer in April 1978 recommended by a new neighborhood friend. "Do you have children?" the attorney asked. "Do you have property to be divided?" Answers of "no" prompted her to say, "This is going to be easy." Not really, I found out. Even when you are the one who wants to get divorced, it's a big deal. I was glad I had made one new friend who had recently divorced and saw that she had survived.

LIFE AT BDC AND BEYOND

As Ian's tenure at BDC went on, his life improved a bit, which basically meant that he wasn't visiting hospital emergency rooms on a regular basis. Ian's seizures were largely controlled with medication, but as a result, he seemed tired much of the time. When I attended an annual or quarterly meeting on Ian's behalf, I asked questions: "Can't you try to decrease the dosage of the medication he's on for epilepsy?" I asked, hoping that I could see echoes of the happy little boy I remembered from years ago. "Can't he have more time in recreation? Is it possible for him to use the pool that's in the main

     Harriet S. Mosatche

building? What's happening with his toilet training? What about getting him appropriate clothing and shoes?" I always had a list of items. Promises were made but were rarely kept.

While Ian was not able to get off the wing independently, other residents navigated the facility on their own. We were often approached by residents who asked us for money so they could use the vending machines in the main building. Our family became friendly with Ray, one of the highest functioning residents. He told us where Ian was and what he was doing, which staff members were kind and which were not. Ray told us of his dream to live in a group home in the community, something that was slowly beginning to happen for some of his peers. Years later, his dream came true, and we were thrilled for him. Tragically, he developed stomach cancer soon after his placement, and within a matter of months he was dead. Although I was sad to learn about Ray's death, I was glad that his wish to live outside an institution had been realized, although for much too short a time.

ANNUAL TREATMENT MEETINGS

Every year family members of BDC residents were invited to the annual treatment team review meetings. Everyone from the social worker to the speech and language pathologist to the wing supervisor attended. If only they spent as much time caring for Ian as they did on the detailed reports they wrote before and after those meetings. The February 1978 report, for instance, included a long list of Ian's skills, such as "points to body parts," "walks briefly on balance board," and "imitates sounds with prompting." Among the many admirable occupational therapy goals on that report were "decrease self-abusive behavior," "increase sitting tolerance," and "improve walking balance and standing balance." The treatment approach included "tactile, vestibular, and proprioceptive" stimulation, which would take the form of "sand box and water play," "simple obstacle runs," and eventually "scooter board activities."

For a moment after these meetings, I felt optimistic about how

Ian would be treated going forward. I am the glass half-full kind of person. But the reality was that we continued to find Ian drugged into oblivion, with fresh bruises on his arms and legs, or asleep in the geriatric chair in front of a blasting TV. Our family tried to make the most of our visits with Ian—playing ball with him, feeding him his favorite foods (even though we continued to be harassed about doing that), and reciting our routines to get a reaction out of Ian, particularly when he was so overmedicated that he could barely hold his head up and drooled onto his shirt. During those visits, it was hard to get Ian to laugh, and sometimes even to smile.

We brought Ian toys that he liked, like pull toys that made clicking noises. But if they were left on his wing, they quickly disappeared. His clothing, too, managed to escape from his closet—Ian Rosenberg labels meant nothing to some staff members who were probably providing outfits to their friends and family. After a while, we stopped bringing clothes and toys to leave on the wing.

THE OUTSIDE ENVIRONMENT

BDC had been built on swampland near a huge landfill of New York City's garbage, which meant that, depending on the direction and strength of the winds, we were treated to nasty odors. However, we still tried to get Ian outside whenever the weather was decent since Ian didn't get out when a family member wasn't around—except for rides to a hospital. Ian liked the change of scenery, and we could be as silly as we wanted. Sometimes, we found an outside bench or a couple of chairs left behind by staff who had taken them outside during their break. When the weather was bad—for us that had to be a temperature of more than 90 and humid or less than 45 degrees or it was pouring (a drizzle was fine), snowing, or hailing—we found space to visit in the main building. Since few families ever visited, we didn't have to compete for indoor space. Although we wanted to take Ian out in colder weather, it was a real challenge as he never kept gloves, mittens, or hats on. Jackets and boots were fine, but Ian found any material below his elbows or on his head a major annoyance. Ian had a habit, taken from our mom, of pushing up his sleeves. While Mom knew to do that only when the weather was warm enough, Ian did not discriminate. As soon as a long-sleeve shirt, sweater, or jacket went on, Ian worked at pushing those sleeves above his elbows. He preferred having limited circulation in his upper arm and freezing fingers to having the sleeves of a long jacket or shirt buttoned at the wrist. One of my strategies was putting a mitten on a hand and then quickly grabbing that covered hand, which gave him a few seconds of warmth until he wiggled his fingers out. Then I changed hands and tried to warm his other hand. Sometimes, I made pulling down his jacket sleeves or putting on his hood into a game—one, two, three down/on (spoken typically with a Russian or German accent that he loved).

Wild dogs often prowled the grounds of BDC. The number, nearness, and threatening nature of the dogs on any particular day determined whether we could actually make it outside and then whether we could stay there. Each building had sand boxes with climbing equipment that had been intended for the residents' recreation, although it was only the dogs that played there. One day as Jay, Marsha, and I headed out with Ian to those sand boxes, I almost stepped onto a sleeping or dead dog. "Dead dog," I yelled to warn the others away. A live dog would have been much more of a threat to us, but "Dead dog" were the words that came out of my mouth, maybe hoping that was the truth. As we ran to safety, Ian chuckled at the unexpected adventure, and we all wound up giggling at the unexpected "dead dog" encounter.

We constantly looked for things to do to keep Ian and us enter-tained during our visits. A large outdoor basketball court was a favorite place to play. No one but our family seemed to use the basketball court. Ian smiled as he watched us play—the constant movement, the groans, the screams of victory. We would help Ian catch the ball and pass it on. He would rub his hands over his ears, as he expressed his joy. We sometimes took Ian to the main building's gym, which he also liked, but it was typically not available to us. Either it was locked or there was some kind of event there (which usually meant more noise and people than Ian could tolerate). And if it wasn't his kind of music (he preferred rock and roll or traditional children's songs), he would grunt and grab until we left. Once in a while the gym was unlocked and empty and we entered quickly and quietly as if we were trespassing, probably because when a guard did find us in there, we were immediately ordered to leave. "For security reasons," we were told. The guards did not appear to be trained to deal compassionately with people with developmental disabilities, or for that matter with any human being. Once when Marsha and I were walking with Ian on the grounds of BDC, a guard grabbed us. "What are you doing here?" he yelled as he reached out to detain us. We quickly explained that we were visiting our brother who lived there and not trespassers or residents.

For a short time, BDC opened a cafeteria in the main building. Freshly made hamburgers and crispy fries were available along with a variety of drinks. Ian loved this food, but I generally didn't have much of an appetite when I visited him (my anxiety over what condition Ian would be in and anticipatory sadness over leaving him at the end of a visit functioned as an easy diet). He liked to tease us with food, picking up a piece and offering it to us, and then as soon as we started to take the piece, he withdrew his hand holding tight onto the morsel until he got it into his mouth. Ian could chew and liked real food, unlike the mush that was served to him on his wing, but because he was always in a rush to get as much food inside his mouth as possible, we cut up his food into small pieces. One of his tricks was swiping several pieces of a cut-up sandwich or a broken up cookie from the plate in front of him, when one of us was not attentive enough. Then Ian would laugh, making the most glorious sound, telling us he had succeeded in outwitting us.

A ROLE MODEL FOR ASSERTIVENESS

Mom always made special cookies or chocolate chip banana bread

 Harriet S. Mosatche

for Ian. She hadn't started to bake, or even cook, until Ian began living at BDC. Grandma had been the one in charge of meals, and since I did not become my grandmother's favorite grandchild until near the end of her life, I always received the smallest portions. Jay and Ian got the most, then Marsha, and then me. Maybe it was because my brothers were boys and to Grandma more valuable. And perhaps Marsha was favored over me because she was named after Grandma's husband Morris, the love of her life, who had died six weeks before Marsha was born. Or maybe it was because I was the only child who acted independently and wasn't afraid to speak back to Grandma when I disagreed with her. She was an incredibly charming woman— I hope I inherited some of that charm. But she was also a force to be reckoned with. Maybe I learned that from her, too, which has served me well over the years as Ian's advocate. No one intimidated Grandma. When President Eisenhower's motorcade drove by on our Brooklyn street, Grandma maneuvered her way to the front of the crowd on the route and greeted him enthusiastically even though she hadn't voted for him. Grandma didn't take nonsense from anyone. When she thought the diaper supply company providing us with Ian's diapers was cheating us, she took the delivery guy aside and told him he was to immediately remove the charge and not step foot in our apartment again. After the man ran out, my gray-haired five foot nothing grandma smacked her hands up and down together, saying, "He won't do anything like that again."

You would think that seeing what Grandma was capable of, I would shy away from conflict with her. But that was not my style. After Grandma told me how to take care of something at home when I was six, I responded, "Don't tell me what to do. You are not my mother." I was typically not a fresh child or a trouble-maker, but I didn't like feeling cornered. Grandma was not pleased by my response, but years later Mom revealed how much she appreciated the way I stood my ground with Grandma since she was hesitant to be assertive at all with her mother. Knitting was my mom's hobby, but when she brought wool home from the yarn store, she hid the bag so that Grandma wouldn't question her. Not that she was using Grandma's money, but Mom couldn't deal with her mother's disapproval, even though she was a grown woman with children of her own. Grandma thought that buying pretty yarns was a luxury we couldn't afford, and when she found a bag of newly bought wool, she had no trouble letting Mom know her that she was shocked by this transgression. Grandma didn't believe Mom's lies about the wool being given to her or having been in the house for months. But for me, it was a relief to see Mom stand up for herself and spend time with her relaxing hobby.

A NEW AGENCY

In 1978 the New York State Office of Mental Retardation and Developmental Disabilities was established, but I never noticed any improvement in Ian's care. In April of that year, Ian was one of 16,447 people residing in one of the state's developmental centers, a number that would decrease as more individuals were moved into community residences or treated in day programs. Later that year, the Site Selection law was passed, providing a framework for creating community housing for people with disabilities. Ian's annual report from that year stated that, "community placement not presently feasible." Although the form allowed for a target date for placement to be filled in, no date was inserted. For item 7e—Criteria for Placement Outside the Facility—the BDC team leader for Ian's case had written in, "elimination of behavioral problems." That meant *never.*

   Harriet S. Mosatche

CHAPTER 11

Good News and Bad

While my marriage to Luc had broken up, Marsha and Steve continued to live a life of wedded bliss, and in 1979, I became an aunt to Sherry who brought much-needed sunshine into our lives. Mom loved to babysit for Sherry while Marsha went back to work for an insurance company, and Dad enjoyed just looking at his grandchild. As a loving aunt who happened to be a developmental psychologist and the sibling of someone who started out as an adorable baby but over time showed the severity of his impairments, I checked Sherry out whenever I saw her. Was she developing normally? Was she alert? Was she reaching developmental milestones at the appropriate ages?

I thought I wanted to become a mom, too, but frankly, I was afraid that my child might be like Ian. No matter how much I loved him, I knew I did not want to bring a child into the world who would always need to be cared for. Not a day went by without feeling worried about Ian. Is someone hurting him? Is he thirsty? Hungry? Does he have a toothache? Is he cold? Too warm? Is his belt tied too tight around his waist? Is he having a seizure?

AIDES—THE EXTRAORDINARY AND THE REST

Although there were a couple of aides who genuinely cared about Ian's welfare, most just wanted him quiet and out of the way so they could watch television or snack without interruption. Mrs. Rivera was the exception. When she was on duty, she recognized when

FINGERPRINTS ON MY HEART   71

Ian wanted food or water, when he was in pain, when he wanted a shower or needed to use the bathroom. We showed our gratitude to her with little gifts and profuse expressions of thanks. Then one day she was no longer working at BDC. I don't know whether she told Ian she was no longer going to be seeing him. And, even if she had, how much would he really understand? I explained to Ian that Mrs. Rivera still loved him but she was no longer able to spend time with him. During each visit, I reminded Ian that our family would continue to visit. Since Mrs. Rivera was no longer in his life, maybe he thought that others he loved would quietly disappear as well.

By the early 1980's when Ian was in his 20's, he was no longer able to walk easily. The injuries from the numerous beatings, the muscle atrophy from inactivity and lack of physical therapy during long hospitalizations and infirmary stays had taken their toll. We began to use a wheelchair to transport him from one place to another. In some ways, that made it easier to take care of Ian who could be extremely stubborn. It runs in the family, I thought, recognizing my similar behavioral patterns. There were times when Ian was still able to walk when he would slide to the ground or on a step in a stairwell and refuse to get up. It would take a fair amount of bribery, usually some kind of sweets to entice him to cooperate. Or a couple of big men to lift him up and get him moving again. Small as he was, he was strong and determined. With Ian in a wheelchair, we could take him out and get him back to his wing using the elevator, without fuss. In the Team Review report for Ian in May 1981, one of the goals listed for placement outside the facility was "will walk between destinations on BDC grounds without sitting for 20 consecutive school days." Another goal was for Ian to "remain in seat cooperatively for a half-hour." Ian could certainly do that if he were given something to do that entertained him—like twine, sand, or food. Of if someone were singing songs he liked or telling him funny stories. But just sitting doing nothing engaging for a half-hour? I couldn't even do that.

    Harriet S. Mosatche

FROM THE PROFESSIONAL TO THE PERSONAL

Professionally, my life was going well. An article I had written with a former student from Hunter College was published in a prestigious journal and evaluations of my teaching performance were excellent (although from time to time, a student would write something like the best part of being in my class was seeing what outfit I was wearing). When I stood in front of the class, nothing interfered with my concentration or performance. I told stories about people I knew to illustrate a difficult concept and focused on the faces of my students so I could change course when I saw hints of boredom. The one person I never talked about in class was Ian. It was just too personal, too close to my heart. And difficult to admit, I was still embarrassed about having a brother with mental retardation. Except when one student came up to me after a session in my Psychology of Exceptional Children class and told me about his brother who had Down Syndrome. I don't know who was more relieved—he or I—as we openly talked about the challenges of having a sibling with a significant cognitive impairment. There were countless times before and after when I kept quiet as colleagues or acquaintances talked about their siblings, not wanting to share my secret life as the sister of a non-verbal young man with a severe cognitive impairment and odd behaviors.

When asked about my siblings, usually I simply talked about Marsha and her normal life. Jay had graduated from college and was devoted to Ian—the center of his life—but he was pathologically shy and did not make an effort to find a job that would have allowed him to live independently. He had shown signs of depression and anxiety for years, but Ian demanded so much attention from my family that little focus was placed on Jay's issues, which were serious but much easier to ignore.

The first man I dated after my divorce from Luc I nicknamed the "Disinhibitor" since he helped me feel comfortable dating again. He patiently waited for me to get over feeling disloyal to Luc when I was with another man. Like me, the Disinhibitor was a psychologist so

I felt safe telling him about Ian, but he was also a synagogue cantor. I loved his singing, but asked him to keep "those religious songs" to a minimum. After I broke up with my Disinhibitor, I dated a number of other men, including some professors—they were so convenient. Since I had become the college advisor to the Class of 1983, I asked various faculty members to join me in chaperoning their dances. Jake was a business professor at Manhattan College who liked dancing as much as I did, and he helped me keep things under control, which was not easy with beer flowing freely from kegs at a time when the legal drinking age was 18. Jake never learned about Ian—we just weren't close enough for me to share that information with him. No point in muddying a fun relationship that we both knew wasn't going any further.

At about that time, I had also taken up a new hobby—jogging—after the head of the physical education department convinced me to sign up for a 10K race in Central Park in New York City. "You'll be a great role model for your students," Laurie said. My new friend Bert (a married biology professor) and I jogged together almost every morning for years, and that was when I told him all my troubles, including the latest incidents at BDC and injuries to Ian. Bert was the kindest man I had ever met, and I could talk to him about everything. He felt the same way about me, and together we discussed and attempted to solve family, college, and world problems. Sometimes, another friend, Lily, joined us, when she wasn't flying to France or India as a flight attendant for the now-defunct airline Pan Am. Our conversations were therapeutic and we did manage to run quickly enough to make our sessions aerobic.

I continued my trek to Brooklyn every other weekend and observed how Grandma's health was deteriorating. She had a couple of strokes and was becoming rather paranoid and confused, signs of her increasing dementia. I wondered how much longer Mom could care for Grandma at home. I volunteered to look into a nursing home that was considered one of the top in the country—some of my students volunteered there since it was right near the col-

     Harriet S. Mosatche

lege campus where I taught. Mom said that she felt guilty, but her mother needed more physical help than she could provide given that was already visiting Ian and taking care of my niece Sherry while Marsha and Steve worked. Once Grandma was moved into the Hebrew Home, my new schedule now included visiting Ian a couple of times a month and seeing Grandma three or four times a week.

CHAPTER 12

A New Man in My Life

As the chair of the Psychology Department at the College of Mount St. Vincent (a position I was appointed to a year after arriving there), I introduced a series of special events during Psychology Week. It was during the hectic days of planning the events that I heard from Ivan, the son of a friend's boss (my friend and Ivan's father worked together for a gourmet food company). I had met Ivan's parents at a food convention a couple of years earlier, having taken advantage of an opportunity for some free samples and more importantly, a chance to meet new people (more specifically, smart, cute men).

MORE THAN A DATE?

Deep into the planning for Psychology Week and working on my first book, I was a little hesitant when Ivan called from Anchorage, Alaska asking me to go out with him on his visit to New York. I liked his parents but did I have the time to meet their son, a man I was never going to see again? Just one night, I reasoned. I didn't really have to attend every event during Psychology Week. Besides, meeting a lawyer working in Alaska intrigued me. He suggested going out to dinner followed by a Broadway show, much nicer than my typical date.

Thursday night arrived. I made sure Dr. Ruth Westheimer's presentation that evening was adequately covered by colleagues—this was just as the sex therapist was gaining popularity with college

 Harriet S. Mosatche

students. When I opened the door that evening, I was surprised to see this tall man wearing a tie and a navy blue blazer, not the professorial worn jeans and plaid shirts I was more accustomed to seeing on men I dated. Ivan and I talked on the car ride into Manhattan, the usual first date kind of stuff. I told him about my job, and we joked about the guest speaker we were missing by going to a show. Our seats were so close to the stage that when the actor Richard Thomas spoke excitedly, his spit landed on our faces. After the show, Ivan asked me whether I wanted to go out dancing. Smart, cute, and a man who liked to dance—too bad he lived over three thousand miles away from me.

After dancing, we went back to my apartment until I finally threw Ivan out at 3 AM. I had classes to teach that day and a Psychology Week event the following evening. Ivan asked to see me on Saturday night, his last day in New York before flying to a Club Med vacation. Our conversation that evening included my predicting that he would be remarried within a couple of years based on a study I had read recently about divorced men in their early 30's—one of the research tidbits I carried around in my head. Ivan told me about some of the strange cases he dealt with as head of the attorney general's office in Anchorage before leaving to join a private practice firm. Again, I thought how unfortunate it was that he lived so far away.

Coming home from work just a few days after Ivan left for his vacation in the Bahamas, I received a letter from him. Although it was flattering to read his words about how I was the kind of woman he'd want to have a long-term relationship with and how he would like to visit me again, I didn't really see the point. We had no possible future together. Still, it was exciting that this man, after two dates, was expressing in a four-page letter how much he had enjoyed his time with me and was now planning to come back to New York instead of heading directly to DC and then on to Alaska—his original plan. We arranged a date for Monday.

THE BALANCE OF LIFE

In our family, when good things happened, we expected misfortune to follow since that kind of balance was part of our history. That October, Marsha was in the last month of her pregnancy, and I couldn't wait to meet my next niece or nephew. I still wasn't sure whether I wanted to take the risk of becoming a mother, but it didn't matter at that point since a likely marriage prospect was not in the picture. Marsha went into the hospital on Saturday for a scheduled Caesarian. I waited at home all day for news about the birth of the new baby in our family. The phone didn't ring. I busied myself working on my book about religious cults. Not a likely topic for a Jewish woman teaching at a Catholic college, but the book offer had come after a publisher had read the write-up in a local newspaper about a talk I had given and thought the time was right—just a couple of years after the mass murders and suicides by cult members in Jonestown, Guyana.

I willed the phone to ring. What's taking so long? When the phone finally rang, the news was horrific. Marsha and Steve's baby girl was stillborn. The autopsy revealed a perfectly formed baby with no discernible cause of death. That night, I cried alone in my apartment. Didn't we already have enough tragedy in our family?

On Monday, Ivan arrived for our date, and at dinner I told him about the stillbirth. I also told him about Ian. As long as I was sharing misfortune, I might as well fill him in on the rest of the family story. We saw each other again on Tuesday and Wednesday nights, and then it was time for Ivan to return to his life and me to mine. We said we would keep in touch. This was 1981—before cell phones, home computers, the Internet, and any inexpensive way to connect. It was not going to be easy.

That weekend, I traveled to Brooklyn. My parents' neighbor Leo, a retired man with a heart condition, had become a regular driver when they visited Ian. Leo liked the gig—he got paid for driving to and from BDC, and we had a reliable, slightly cheaper form of transportation than car service. I was glad that Leo would some-

 Harriet S. Mosatche

times get out of the car and spend a little time with us during our visit with Ian. He was one of the very few people who didn't treat Ian as if his cognitive impairment were contagious. But I worried that Leo would have a heart attack while driving us. I instructed whoever was sitting in the passenger seat next to Leo what to do in case he showed any sign of keeling over. Not that I knew how to drive, but I figured that grabbing the steering wheel and putting on the emergency brake would be better than allowing the car to move totally unattended.

Although we had been using a wheelchair for some time to more easily transport Ian, I noticed that each time I visited Ian that fall and winter, he had even more trouble walking. His right foot had become twisted and swollen and his leg muscles showed signs of atrophy. Ian made the best of his situation; when he was in too much pain to put pressure on his feet, he scooted around on the floor.

IT'S GETTING SERIOUS

Right around Thanksgiving, Ivan called me from Alaska (his phone bills were mounting), and at some point during that conversation, he said: "I love you." I was shocked, since we had only seen each other five times, and I took that phrase very seriously. I did not respond with "I love you, too." I knew I cared about Ivan and wanted to continue to have some kind of relationship with him but love was too big a feeling for me at that time. "That's nice to know," I feebly replied. After that conversation, every time we spoke, Ivan told me he loved me, and I awkwardly responded with either a "Thank you" or "That's nice." Love meant that you wanted to spend your life with that person. Didn't Ivan get that? Next came Ivan's request that I meet him in Cincinnati for Christmas, where his parents and other relatives gathered each year. Since he didn't offer to pay for the plane trip, I had to consider whether I wanted to spend some of my hard-earned meager salary on a ticket to see this man I really liked, but with whom I could not see a future. After discussing the situation with Mom as well as with friends and colleagues, I bought a ticket on a discount airline. Ivan said he would pick me up at the airport and then said: "I'm not sure I'll recognize you." "What? He tells me he loves me but can't remember what I look like?" I thought. "I'll be wearing a red coat," I told him.

Our time together that Christmas was like the scenes from a romantic movie—walking through the Cincinnati zoo lit up at night, dining at one of the country's best restaurants, slow dancing to my favorite song, "Lady in Red," and swimming in the pool at the hotel. Of course, we put in appearances, when necessary, at the homes of relatives. Since we had to fly back to our respective cities before the first of the year, we bought a bottle of champagne and pretended that December 27 was New Year's Eve. Ivan gave me a jewelry box and a round-trip ticket to Alaska, which he later mentioned he was only going to give me if our visit went well. A very practical man. By the time I flew back to my life in New York, I was in love and no longer hesitant about saying so.

IVAN MEETS MY FAMILY

When Western Airlines inaugurated its service between New York and Alaska with a great sale, Ivan bought ten round-trip tickets. Those tickets would either nourish our relationship at a good price or he would return them—no risk at all. As I've said before, he's a practical man. I wanted Ivan to meet both Grandma and Ian. Not that these were tests of how serious he was about us or how he accepted my family. Well, maybe they were tests. He didn't seem to have a great relationship with his parents, and I had been disappointed by how impatient he was with them when we were all together at Christmas. I had a lot more to learn about Ivan.

On Ivan's February visit to New York, I took him to meet Grandma at the Hebrew Home. Ivan ignored the inappropriate behavior around him—the cursing, the yelling, the attempts to undress in public. A nurse told us that Grandma was sitting outside on the patio. Although I had told Grandma about Ivan, she didn't really remember too much those days. I introduced them, and at

 Harriet S. Mosatche

some point, Ivan asked her whether she knew what kind of work I did. "I'm not sure, but I know she's a big shot," Grandma responded. I laughed as Ivan said: "That's true." As we were leaving, Ivan told her that he looked forward to seeing her again soon. Unlike the way Ivan acted with his parents, he showed patience with Grandma—good signs for a future with this man.

Since the weekend Ivan was in town I was also scheduled to visit Ian, I planned to introduce the two of them. Ivan drove us to Brooklyn, first to pick up my parents (who were also meeting Ivan for the first time) and then on to BDC. I was always nervous before visiting Ian, wondering what kind of condition he would be in, but this time, I was anxious about how Ivan and Ian would interact. Ivan had done well with Grandma, but I was sure he had never met anyone like Ian, nor had he experienced an institution like BDC. Unlike my usual visits to BDC, I arrived without feeling exhausted—what a pleasure to make that trip by car. Ian was in the area with the television, although he was not facing it. I told Ian that I wanted him to meet my boyfriend Ivan from Alaska. Ian seemed to like the sound of the word "Alaska" and grabbed Ivan's sweater gently when Ivan approached him. We walked with Ian into his bedroom with Ian a little unsteady and holding on to me for support.

My father was not embarrassed telling Ian the Willie Dreshen story in front of Ivan, but I couldn't bring myself to use the German or Russian accent that Ian enjoyed with my boyfriend present. My relationship with Ivan was too new for me to make a fool of myself in front of him. Ian smiled when I told him about the algebra class story with Jill as the committed Communist, but he knew something was missing. Ivan talked quietly to Ian briefly about living in Alaska—the snow, the bears, the moose. But Ivan didn't know yet that the key to Ian's enjoyment of a story was an exaggerated accent and a loud voice.

This was the first time since Luc that I had brought a man to visit Ian. While Tim, one of my boyfriends after Luc, sometimes picked me up from my parents' house after a visit home, I had not asked him to visit Ian with me. Taking Ivan to visit Ian at BDC signaled to my parents the serious nature of our relationship. Mom, knowing little about Ivan's life as a practicing attorney in cosmopolitan Anchorage, Alaska, gave Ivan the nickname of Musher. Ian smiled when he heard Mom refer to Ivan by that name, but I didn't share the nickname with Ivan—not right away at least.

JUST VISITING

That April, I used the plane ticket Ivan had given me to visit him in Alaska. It was my spring break from teaching, and I took my lucky red wool coat—the one I had worn to meet Ivan in Cincinnati—with me on that trip. A couple of days after arriving, I saw the headline on the first page of the Anchorage Daily News: "Blizzard Hits Northeast." The sky was blue, and the weather was mild that day in Anchorage. The newspaper stand was right outside the deli where Ivan had arranged for us to have lunch. A photo showed snow piled high. "Ivan has outdone himself," I thought. He had a newspaper made up to show an April snowstorm in New York City. Ivan had to work hard to convince me that he had nothing to do with the news. A freak storm really had struck the northeast, and I called home to make sure my family was safe. I always worried about Ian on days like that. Would staff make it to BDC in that weather? Would there be enough people supervising the residents?

As my Alaska vacation came to an end, I broke the news to Ivan that I wouldn't ever move to his state. My family needed me too much, so I had to stay in New York. How could Ian survive without my regular visits and my advocacy? Who would visit Grandma to make sure she was taken care of? Ivan loved me, but he loved his life in Alaska, too. I got on the plane back to New York, not knowing where our relationship was headed.

The weekend I returned to New York, I visited Ian at BDC and found some scratches on his arms and legs, but not enough to make a fuss. His broad smile told me how much he had missed me. He

     Harriet S. Mosatche

made the noise of an airplane flying through the air as I told him about my long trip. I knew that I did love Ivan, and yet I would miss Ian and the rest of the family too much to leave.

I was surprised that Ivan didn't call for a few days after I returned. I knew he was busy, but something else was up. I called him, and there was something different about the tone of our conversation. During our visit I had asked him to commit to moving to New York to be with me, and he wasn't ready to do that. How could Alaska hold more of an allure than me? He was the one who had pushed our relationship forward, I reminded him. I didn't need a wedding date, I had told him when I was visiting Alaska. I just wanted to know that we had a future together. Ivan said that he thought that once I visited him in Alaska and saw his life there, I would feel comfortable with the idea of moving. At no time had I given Ivan any encouragement for thinking that way. I felt betrayed. I had just turned 33, and my biological clock was ticking. Yes, I had changed my mind about having children—I wanted to have them and Ivan was the man I wanted as their father. Spending time with my niece Sherry and seeing the normal children of my faculty peers had convinced me that I couldn't allow Ian's disability to prevent me from experiencing parenthood.

I needed to decide how I would react, knowing it would be hard for Ivan to give up a life he loved, but recognizing that it would be impossible for me to leave my family. Push Ivan who was already feeling cornered or give him lots of space and time to figure out what he wanted? Although I have a strong need for control—not surprising given my family circumstances—I stopped pushing for a definite answer. I wasn't going to wait indefinitely, but I decided to wait for a while to see what would unfold.

CHAPTER 13

The Wilds of Alaska and Brooklyn

My life was busy with work, trips to see Ian, visits to Grandma, letters and cards to Ivan (we wrote to each other every day in this pre-Internet era), and phone calls with him (usually in the middle of the night for me since Ivan rarely got home before 9 PM and Alaska was five hours behind New York at that time). Two colleagues and I applied for a grant from the National Institutes of Health for a project on adult sibling relationships. It is not surprising that this topic became a research interest of mine. Colleagues told us that we were unlikely to get a major government grant without a history of smaller grants, so I began to look into summer teaching positions in Anchorage. Ivan really wanted me to do that, and I thought that my family might be able to cope with my being away for six weeks. I greeted the news that we had received the NIH grant with mixed feelings—excited that our proposal had been funded, disappointed that my plan to spend most of the summer with Ivan was no longer possible, and somewhat relieved that I wouldn't be away from Ian for so long.

The work on the grant went smoothly that summer; we developed research instruments and trained several students (including one who is a dear friend today) to conduct comprehensive interviews with adults ranging from their 20's to their 70's. Our focus was on how siblings could support each other, substituting for

Harriet S. Mosatche

care that would otherwise need to be provided by government and other agencies. My own sibling Marsha became one of our research assistants, coding the interviews into the categories we developed to represent the many roles siblings play in each other's life.

A TEMPER TANTRUM

I figured out how I could take a break from the intense work required by the grant for three weeks at the end of the summer. My plan included visiting Ian the weekend before flying to Alaska for three weeks and then visiting him again as soon as I returned. Although that was a longer period than I had ever stayed away, it was the best I could do. Starting out early on Saturday morning, I arrived at my parents' house, and we took car service together to BDC. Jay joined us that day. As usual, my pulse raced a bit as we walked through the main building to get to Ian's wing, hoping to find Ian in decent condition. Jay walked quickly ahead as my parents and I slowly made our way to Ian's building. When I saw Jay walking back to us, my immediate thought was: "What happened to Ian now?"

"You just missed him," Jay said. "Ian is going on a trip."

"He never goes anywhere, why today?" I asked, not expecting an answer.

"I was able to get on the bus before it left. I told him to have a good time," Jay said. Although a very small part of me was glad that Ian was finally going someplace other than to a hospital, I started to cry with frustration. I had missed seeing Ian by mere minutes. After almost three hours of traveling, I was not going to see Ian that day or for the next four weeks. Six weeks all together.

"Why hadn't I walked ahead with Jay?" I thought. I felt like screaming, how unfair the world was.

Mom tried to help me see things rationally. "Be happy that Ian is on a trip and having a good time. When I see him next, I'll tell him you were here, and that you're in Alaska visiting the Musher."

I was inconsolable, like a two-year-old having a temper tantrum. No one was going to make me feel better about not seeing Ian that day. I had timed things perfectly so that my time in Alaska would mean four weeks away from Ian. Now that had stretched to six weeks, which seemed like more than Ian or I could deal with. Maybe I shouldn't have agreed to spend three weeks with Ivan. I felt guilty and I hadn't even gotten on the plane yet.

Happily, my three weeks in Alaska were filled with adventure. We explored Denali Park (where we spotted bears and moose), Homer (where our hotel room inexplicably had a towel bar attached to the ceiling), and Valdez (where we enjoyed a delicious salmon bake). It seemed to me that Ivan was still trying to convince me that I would have a wonderful life in Alaska, but I knew that I would never change my mind. My family needed me too much. And if I could break down about missing Ian for a few weeks, how could I cope with leaving him behind in New York to start a life in Alaska.

A NEW BEGINNING AND AN END

Apparently, Ivan had gotten the message. In September Ivan called and told me that he had been offered a position with a New York law firm. My cousin Rona's husband Marty (Ian's lawyer) worked for that firm and had gotten Ivan an interview. Ivan told me that when he told his father about the job offer, his dad had asked: "So when are you getting married?"

"So when are we?" Ivan asked me.

"Is that a proposal?" I asked.

"I guess so," said the practical man.

Ivan arranged to leave his job in Anchorage in early December and began to pack up his life in Alaska.

By early December Grandma's health had further deteriorated, having fractured her hip in a fall followed by a series of strokes. She spent almost all of her time in bed, and when I visited, she said only one thing, "I want to die." Each time I visited, I sang her favorite song, the one her husband used to sing to her: "When Your Hair

     Harriet S. Mosatche

Has Turned to Silver."

My friend and jogging partner Bert advised me that I needed to let Grandma know that it was okay for her to die. When I next visited, I told Grandma it was okay to let go, that we would all be fine, that she was a wonderful grandmother, and that I loved her very much. I sang her song for her and walked out of the room. Two days later, my secretary said that someone from my grandmother's nursing home was on the phone. Grandma had died, just a few days before Ivan was scheduled to arrive in New York. Sorrow was mixed with relief—Grandma had been so miserable, but her death still left me feeling sad.

Ivan and I married a couple of months after he moved to New York, but not before the apartment I had found for us was totally burglarized. After Ivan's furniture arrived from Alaska, we had about two days to wonder what we would do with the two televisions we now owned. The burglary solved that problem. Both were taken along with almost everything else of value. While some of our stolen belongings could easily be replaced, I was sad to lose a ring and a watch given to me by the grandmother who had just died. On the other hand, I wasn't heartbroken when Ivan's wedding ring from his first marriage was found to be among the pieces now lost forever. Unfortunately, the engagement ring from my marriage to Luc was left behind by the thieves. Couldn't they have looked a little harder? That was the one thing I wouldn't have minded getting stolen, particularly since it was separately and adequately insured.

We had a small wedding in February 1983, a week after a blizzard paralyzed New York, and with the heating system at the restaurant broken, our guests had to stand around an electric heater—all fitting for a groom who had just left Alaska. Our three-day honeymoon in the Catskills Mountains was all we had time for since I had to get back to teaching and Ivan, new to his position, certainly couldn't take off any time yet. We bought a car, and although I now had a driver's license (which I thought was more of an accomplishment than earning my Ph.D.), Ivan was the one driving us to Brooklyn every other weekend.

MORE BRUISES, VIVID DOCUMENTATION

Along with lots of memorabilia I saved are photos of Ian from the winter of 1982-1983. Ivan had told us that we should make sure to have the first page of a newspaper showing in each photo of Ian taken when he was bruised to document that the injuries could not have happened before that date. A couple of the photos show Ian laying in a hospital bed with bruises all over his legs. Another shows a hospital gown pulled up to reveal several large contusions along Ian's spine. One of the most heartbreaking photos is a close-up of Ian's face, with a swollen and discolored eye, with Mom's hand holding a newspaper with the headline, "Spend More Gas For Area Homes" from the 15-cent *New York Daily News*.

BDC staff always explained away those deep scratches on his back and black and blue bruises on his legs, arms and face. Maybe staff were negligent and not vigilant enough to prevent Ian from being hurt by another resident or even by himself. An even more sinister possibility was that Ian was being abused by staff. Since Ian couldn't speak, we couldn't prove anything. Ivan prepared an affidavit for my parents to sign that gave Ivan and me access to Ian's records so we could act in a more official capacity on behalf of Ian—going to meetings, writing letters, and asking administrators for information. Our family continued to be one of the most active families of a BDC resident. Although we saw our role as Ian's advocate, some staff saw us as constant annoyances. While I usually cared about what people thought of me and wanted to be liked, when it came to Ian's care I was happy to be a pest.

Ian's May 1983 quarterly report included the following requirements for Ian to be placed outside BDC:

> *Ian will increase peer interaction in a group setting while in the classroom.*
> *Ian will brush his hair independently.*
> *Ian will complete a 25-piece round peg board independently.*
> *Ian will wash his hands with soap and water upon request.*

 Harriet S. Mosatche

Ian clearly had a lot of work to do to be ready for a move to a community facility. Since Ian did not understand the connection between reaching these goals and getting to live in a group home, he was not motivated to make the required changes in his behavior. However, he could make the connection between engaging in a requested behavior and being rewarded for it with something he really wanted. Although I repeatedly offered staff numerous suggestions about the kinds of things that might work as rewards for Ian, I wasn't optimistic that staff would follow up.

By December of 1983, 11,728 people were living in developmental centers, and 12,100 were residing in the community in "group homes" in the state of New York. Getting Ian moved out of BDC and into community housing was our goal. Achieving that was a lot harder than we originally thought.

Now that Ivan was Ian's lawyer, Ivan began to keep records of his observations from each meeting, phone call, and visit. Not that we were planning to sue, but we needed clear documentation about Ian's care and condition to help us advocate for him. From our visit on February 12, 1984, Ivan wrote: "Ian had a terrible rash on his buttocks. He also had a rash on his ankles." Two weeks later, Ivan wrote: "Ian still had a rash on his buttocks. Also, he had a jumpsuit on backwards so that the back of his collar was putting pressure on his neck." In early March, the notes read: "Multiple scratches on his right forearm; scratches on his right cheek, scratch above his left eye and on the left side of his nose. Multiple scratches on the back of his neck." An administrator, Mr. B, noted that there were several incident reports over the past couple of months, including one that described Ian being hit by a chair hurled by a resident during mealtime. When Ivan questioned Mr. B about the way Ian was often restrained, the administrator admitted that he has to work with existing staffing and that "perhaps" Ian's civil rights were being violated. Perhaps?

CHAPTER 14

New Job, New Life, and News Reports

After the publication of my first book in early 1984, I decided to look for a new job. I needed a position that would pay more than the wages I was getting from the small Catholic college where the running joke among faculty was that while the nuns had taken a vow of poverty, we should not have to. After six years of serving as department chair and earning tenure, it was time to move on. I wanted my career to go in a different direction that would involve more writing and not just the academic kind. My book, *Searching*, about religious cults and human potential movements had lit a fire under me—writing for the public could have an impact and could give me recognition. Not sure of what I was looking for, I searched the classified section of *The New York Times*, a common way for people to find jobs in the 1980's.

GAIN AND LOSS

A position in the Program Development department of Girl Scouts of the USA, described in *The New York Times*, intrigued me. I knew nothing about that organization, except for my experience attending one Girl Scout meeting when I was 10. As a young girl in a family with limited financial resources, finding out about the "requirement" (which I learned 24 years later was not true) to purchase a uniform immediately closed the door on membership. At

 Harriet S. Mosatche

that age, I had never owned a new article of clothing. Reviewing the job requirements, I realized that I was a perfect fit, not just something I needed to say in a cover letter. The position offered many opportunities for me to write and to use my expertise on behalf of girls. After going through the application and interview process, a job offer was made, and I accepted. I finished teaching my last courses in early May 1984 and soon after that completed my faculty responsibilities.

That month, a front-page article in *The New York Times* appeared with the title, "Mental Patients Reported Abused at Queens Center." The content of the article didn't surprise me. "Evidence of wide-spread abuse—including the beating of mentally ill patients with blackjacks and bamboo poles—has been uncovered in a special ward of the Creedmoor Psychiatric Center in Queens, according to state investigators," wrote reporter Philip Shenon. The article went on to state, "Such abuse…might have been prevented had the staff been better trained and more closely supervised, according to investigators for the panel, the State Commission on Quality of Care for the Mentally Disabled." I knew that Creedmoor was not the only institution with that problem. I placed that article in a file labeled "Ian," a folder that kept growing with notes written on tiny pieces of paper, letters I received in response to my inquiries, and articles related to the care or more often the abuse of those who had disabilities.

In early July 1984, soon after starting my new job, I became pregnant. Ivan and I both wanted children, and seeing how healthy and happy my niece Sherry was, my fear about giving birth to a child with a severe disability had eased. My parents and Ivan's were excited about the news. I didn't want to tell my boss until my pregnancy became more obvious. There would be plenty of time to share the news at work

While I suffered from morning sickness that lasted 24/7, Ivan and I continued to visit Ian every other week. I kept my supply of bread sticks readily available since when I ate them the nausea lessened. Ivan's notes from our visit to Ian on August 19, 1984 read: "2 PM. Ian had scabs on both nostrils. He had two socks on each hand taped very tightly with elastic bands biting into his wrists. Skin on the inside of his left wrist was rubbed raw from the socks. His trousers were taped at the top. He hadn't been changed since the night shift, according to the day shift. He had deep healing scratches on his back—two on the left side and two near his spine."

On Monday, Ivan and I were back at work, back to our regular routine. I was planning to keep my job after a brief maternity leave. That was the plan. Until the day ten weeks into the pregnancy when I began to have severe abdominal pains and some bleeding. As the day turned into night, the pain and bleeding became more intense until I expelled the sac holding the tiny fetus into the toilet. All I could do was cry and clean every household surface—trying to rub away the pain of losing my baby. I told myself that miscarriages prevent the birth of a baby who would otherwise be born severely deformed, who carried abnormal genes, who would have a miserable existence. But then I realized how much I loved Ian in spite of his disability. I would have loved my baby, no matter what, I thought. But did I really want a child to suffer the way Ian did?

After my doctor performed a D and C procedure to clean out my uterus, I sobbed. A dream, not just our baby, was dead. When I got home, I cleaned some more—the stove was more spotless than it had ever been before. That evening, a former student (now a close friend) who had applied for a job as a nanny, called to ask me to serve as a reference. Although I knew she would be perfect for that position, I refused. I couldn't talk about anything related to children. And for weeks afterwards, I hated seeing pregnant women and babies in strollers. They were everywhere.

REVEALING NEWS REPORTS

Just a week after my miscarriage, an article in *The New York Times* on Sunday, September 23, 1984 caught my attention. In "State Agrees to Changes at L.I. Center for Retarded" Joseph P. Fried

    Harriet S. Mosatche

wrote that New York State would "take the many steps the judge ordered to end shortcomings he had found in the provision of food, clothing, medical care, building maintenance, sanitary conditions and training programs at the 465-acre, 19-year-old institution." The lawsuit that led to the ruling was brought by residents and parents of residents who were concerned about the "severe inadequacies" at the state-run Suffolk Developmental Center in Melville, Long Island. That's exactly what I had been seeing for years at Brooklyn Developmental Center.

On October 14, 1984, another relevant article appeared in *The New York Times*. The same commission that had investigated Creedmoor Hospital reported "widespread mismanagement" in the Niagara County Association for Retarded Children's group homes and programs. Although the Commission on Quality of Care for the Mentally Disabled noted that the problems had been corrected, "these failures are cited as dramatic illustrations of the consequences of ineffective regulation." Among the instances cited were: "failure to protect the retarded from physical abuse and the covering up of incidents of abuse" and "poor nutritional programs for the retarded and chronic food shortages." The same kinds of problems, I knew, were happening all over the country, not just in New York. Horrified as I was by reports of abuse and neglect visited on those who couldn't protect themselves, I was glad to finally see real, public attention paid to issues that I had cared about and tried unsuccessfully to rectify–at least for Ian—for years. At the Democratic National Convention in 1984, Senator Ted Kennedy, whose sister Rosemary had cognitive impairments, spoke movingly about disability rights, and increased public recognition of this issue.

TRYING AGAIN

Life went on, and in January of 1985, I had the green light for trying to get pregnant again. Now I was worried not just about whether my child would be normal but also whether I would have another miscarriage. In early February I started jury duty and was quickly assigned to serve on a bank robbery case. Evidently I had gotten pregnant right before my jury service began. I started feeling nauseous and missed my period, but I didn't visit the doctor until the bank robbery case was over. Although I could have asked to be excused from the jury once the intense nausea began since there were alternates, I was afraid to leave the decision in the hands of a jury that I recognized could not be trusted to arrive at a fair and well-informed verdict. As foreperson, I felt a strong obligation to see the case through to its conclusion. Arriving at a "Guilty" verdict for two of the defendants was easy for all of us. But I fought hard to keep two others from spending the better part of their lives in prison because one juror was anxious about going on a planned vacation while others were convinced that only guilty people are charged with crimes. The case concluded with a hung jury for the remaining two defendants, which was the best I could hope for since I was unable to convince people who didn't understand the judge's instructions or believed that guilt by association was a valid reason for conviction.

Throughout my pregnancy, we visited Ian regularly, and, as before, always with a good supply of bread sticks on hand to deal with my ever-present "morning sickness." Once my pregnancy had become very obvious, Ivan and I told Ian our news. "You're going to be an uncle," we told him. It was impossible to know how much Ian understood, but he would touch my shirt, sometimes laughing as he picked it up when we talked about the baby growing inside me. Luckily, this pregnancy progressed well, and I looked forward to the birth of my first child.

With Ian's mobility becoming more limited and his leg muscles atrophying, we pressed for regular physical therapy. We were told that while physical therapists had been authorized, BDC hadn't been able to hire anyone because of its location and the type of residents. Soon Ian could no longer walk or stand without assistance, and he spent most of his time in a wheelchair. We now had something new to complain about—the poor condition of Ian's

     Harriet S. Mosatche

wheelchair. Two physical therapy consultants were called in by the BDC administration to evaluate the condition of Ian's wheelchair and make recommendations to support his safety. Their report from September 30, 1985, less than two weeks before my son Robert's birth, recommended the following:

1. *Seat belt must be repaired on Ian's wheelchair. In Ian's case, lack of a seatbelt is a significant safety hazard.*
2. *Foot rests with ankle straps should be provided for Ian's wheelchair. This absence also represents a safety hazard.*
3. *Wheelchair evaluation with eye toward increasing seat height to facilitate proper positioning when foot rests are provided.*

The report said exactly what we had requested, but evidently the two consultants had no more power than we did. Nothing improved and our nagging continued.

When Robert was about six weeks old, we decided to take him with us on our visit to Ian. We picked up Mom and Dad. While Robert didn't have a clue as to where we were or who Ian was, Ian looked at Robert with curiosity and smiled. Keeping my distance from Ian with Robert in my arms, I told Ian that Robert was the baby who had been inside me. Ian touched my shirt to tell me he understood. But he probably thought I was still pregnant since, unlike those celebrity new moms showing off their taut abs two weeks after giving birth, I still looked as if I were in my last trimester. We kept the visit short since we had a long trip back—to drop my parents off at their home and then on to New Rochelle where we now lived. Not wanting Ian to be jealous of Robert, I asked Ivan to hold him while I performed my Mr. Schmendrick routine, which I knew Ian would laugh at and would reassure him that a baby wouldn't change our relationship.

I returned to work after a six-week maternity leave, and Mom and Dad lived with us during the week to care for Robert. We tried to visit Ian twice a month, but sometimes the weather or Robert being ill—he had constant ear infections that first winter—interfered with our plans. I always felt guilty when that happened even though I knew my brother Jay would let us know if we needed to follow up on anything untoward.

Bringing Robert with us to visit Ian was a way to demonstrate to our child that Ian was part of our family, that he was not someone to be afraid of. However, since Ian didn't understand his strength or a baby's fragility, we had to keep Robert away from Ian's reach. When Ivan held Rob aloft like an airplane, zooming him in to get close (but not too close) to Ian, both laughed. I watched the scenario with joy—three important guys in my life enjoying this game together.

PROMISING TREND

A ruling by the U. S. Supreme Court in 1985 gave me renewed hope for Ian's future. The decision in City of Cleburne v. Cleburne Living Center was that localities could not use zoning laws to prevent the establishment of group homes for individuals with developmental disabilities merely because the residents had disabilities. More importantly, the case made people with disabilities a semi-protected class. The momentum for acceptance of people like my brother seemed to be building.

Although neither Ivan nor I went to Ian's care plan meetings in 1985 or 1986, I did review the goals that staff set for him along with his accomplishments as described in the reports of those meetings. I was surprised to read that as of March 18, 1986, Ian had obviously achieved some key tasks such as: "Can work at a task for 30 minutes with physical prompts; can hold hands with another client; can plug the electrical cord into an outlet with hand-to-hand assistance." While I understood why persisting at a task and holding hands with peers was valuable, I didn't get the importance of a goal related to electricity. With Robert having just turned five months old, I was busy child-proofing the house, particularly focusing on getting plastic inserts into every outlet. With all the tasks that could have

     Harriet S. Mosatche

helped Ian develop his fine motor skills, why would they choose one that could encourage Ian to experiment with a live outlet? Also puzzling in the report recommendations to prepare Ian for placement outside BDC was the goal for him "to shave his face." So, if he didn't manage to electrocute himself by playing with the outlet, he could try cutting up his face with a razor. Giving staff the benefit of the doubt, shaving probably would be done with an electric razor.

CHAPTER 15

A Changing Landscape

While Ian loved to listen to the same routines and knew when to point to his legs or head to fill in his part, we tried out different routines from time to time, partly to find new ways to entertain Ian but also to reduce our boredom from endlessly repeating the same story.

NEW ROUTINES DIRECT FROM ALASKA

When Ivan became part of our family, he brought with him stories, lots of them. And they could be embellished with accents and dramatic phrasing. While Ivan's theater experience began and ended in high school, he was a litigator, a bit of a ham, and, most important, not afraid to act foolishly to make Ian laugh. One of Ian's favorite Ivan stories involved Magda, a woman who had cleaned Ivan's condo in Alaska when she wasn't telling him about her weekend adventures with her husband Kurt. Fortunately, they were German-born with thick accents, Ian's favorite kind of accent, so all Ivan had to do was imitate them faithfully. Ian's favorite Magda story went like this:

Oh, Ivan, you can't imagine what happened last weekend when Kurt and I drove our car across the lake to our cabin on a little island. We were just talking when suddenly we heard a cracking noise. Oh no! Could that be the ice starting to break? I was sooo scared. I didn't know whether we were going to make it to the island. Kurt began sweating, and I started praying. We kept driving slowly, slowly across the lake while those cracking sounds continued. Thank God, we made it to the cabin.

I don't know how much of the story Ian really understood, but Ivan's imitation of Magda made all of us laugh, particularly when he talked about Kurt "svetting."

Another story Ivan told came from much earlier in his life, from his days as an eighth-grader when he had a Latin teacher who was old enough to have also taught many of the parents of his classmates. For this story, Ivan used a southern accent spoken in a "sing-songy" high-pitched, old lady voice.

Ivan pointed to Ian pretending to be Mrs. Goren talking to one of the new students in her class: *Peter, didn't your father go to Walnut Hills? I taught him waaaay back in 1948.*

Ivan then points to me: *What about you, Melissa? Your mother was in my class in 1946. She was very smart but a real troublemaker. I hope you won't be like that.*

Ian's enjoyment seemed to have more to do with the accent, voice pitch, and strange-sounding words than it had to do with the actual content of the story. However, from time to time Ian indicated his understanding of sophisticated comments. When I used the word "pregnant," Ian would grab my shirt and smile, showing me that he knew what that word meant. I can only imagine how frustrated he must have been to not be able to express himself in a way that others could understand. When Ian pointed to his arm, for instance, I had to guess at what he meant. He made it clear when I guessed wrong by grunting, but when I really couldn't figure it out, I would sometimes just pretend that I had figured out what he meant. That seemed to satisfy him. Or maybe he was just humoring me.

Since Dad was finding it increasingly more difficult to visit Ian regularly because of his debilitating arthritis, Ivan became the substitute teller of the Willie Dreshen story. Ivan had heard the story more than a hundred times. He was prepared and added his own touches to the story. It didn't simply end with: "I blew my nose and now I talk like this."

Ivan added the following line: "But the girl still wouldn't dance with me because I was such a nerd." Ian recognized the change in the story, his face showing some puzzlement when he first heard that new ending. I don't think Ian knew what a nerd was, but his grin showed us that he appreciated Ivan's creativity and effort to enhance the story. Ivan also added me to the story by stating that Willie Dreshen's psychology professor was none other than Dr. Mosatche. When asked who Dr. Mosatche was, Ian pointed to me.

Ian never let us end a visit without someone reciting the Willie Dreshen story. Ian would touch his nose, which signified Willie Dreshen's nasal voice, and he wouldn't stop until he heard the whole story. Usually, Ian heard only one rendition of the Willie Dreshen story on any visit. I was concerned that if he heard it more frequently, it would become less special over time and stop bringing him so much joy. The exception we made was when Ian was in the hospital or in obvious pain, and the Willie Dreshen story was the surest way we could think of to lessen his distress.

SOME THINGS CHANGE, OTHERS DON'T

By the time Robert turned a year old, Mom said she could no longer care for him while I was working a full-time schedule. While she adored her grandson, she felt a strong need to return to her life and responsibilities in Brooklyn. Instead of looking for day care or a babysitter for Robert, I decided to leave my job. Much as I liked my work at Girl Scouts—and the income—I focused on the positives in my new situation: no more twice-weekly round-trips to and from Brooklyn to take my parents' home and back to our house; more privacy for Ivan and me; and most important, more time with my son. For the next couple of years, I did freelance writing projects when Robert napped or when Ivan was home. I made friends with

     Harriet S. Mosatche

other neighborhood mothers who had children close in age to Robert. We talked about toilet training, temper tantrums, and husbands. They talked about their siblings, and I shared stories about Marsha. My life with Ian stayed safe in that private compartment I had created. And I rarely talked about Jay since he, too, was not a normal sibling, with his extreme shyness having turned him into someone with a rich fantasy world but no job and just a couple of friends whom he rarely saw.

We continued to keep track of the injuries Ian sustained and to complain to BDC administrators. In August of 1986, my parents received a detailed document, the Residents' Bill of Rights, from BDC's director, as required by regulations from the New York State Department of Health as well as the federal Department of Health and Human Services. Item 5 stated:

> *The resident will be free from mental and physical abuse, and free from chemical and physical restraints, except as follows:*
>
> *Restraints may only be applied if alternative techniques have failed (such failure is to be documented in the resident's records) and only if such restraints impose the least possible restriction consistent with their purposes.*
>
> *Only professionals designated by the Director may order the use of restraints. Such orders shall be in writing and shall not be in force for over four hours. A resident placed in restraints shall be checked at least every thirty minutes by staff trained in the use of restraints and a written record of such checks shall be kept. Mechanical restraints shall be designed for minimum discomfort and used so as not to cause physical injury to the residents. Opportunity for motion and exercise shall be provided for a period of not less than ten minutes during each two hours in which restraints are employed.*

It sounded so good on paper, but Ian at age 28 continued to be restrained in a variety of ways, from mittens placed around his hands and taped to his arms, which prevented him from freely moving his fingers, or the "geriatric chair," which was positioned with a tray held tight against his chest that didn't allow him to maneuver around the floor. If we had a better option, we would have moved Ian, but our research confirmed that other developmental centers suffered from similar abuse and neglect. To our great distress and frustration, in the 1980's, this was still the norm.

Then there was Item 12 of the 12-point Bill of Rights, which stated the following: "The resident shall be treated with consideration, respect, and full recognition of his dignity and individuality, including privacy in treatment and in care for his personal needs." It if were not so crushingly sad, this would have been laughable. I've tried hard to remember instances in which Ian was treated with respect and dignity. From time to time, a staff member after Mrs. Rivera left showed some consideration for Ian's welfare and an understanding of his humanity—calling him by name, touching him in a caring way, complimenting him for responding to a command. But most of the time, upon entering Ian's wing I found him asleep or in a dazed state near the front desk restrained in a geriatric chair. Nobody was paying attention to him or to any other resident, the music played so loudly that it had to be a violation of OSHA regulations, and staff were talking together or folding laundry.

On September 17, 1987, Willowbrook Developmental Center (an institution that had been widely publicized for its despicable treatment of its residents) was officially closed. Plans were in the works for the centers in the Bronx and Manhattan to close, but BDC remained open. At about that time, Dad and Mom decided it was time to leave Brooklyn to live closer to us. My parents had been finding it increasingly difficult to take care of their house, and we lived too far from them to easily remedy whatever issues came up. And problems were cropping up far too regularly. Dad could no longer navigate the stairs with his severe arthritis. We found a condo

     Harriet S. Mosatche

apartment for my parents and Jay, who still lived at home with them, that was just about a 10-minute drive away from our house.

ANOTHER CHILD

That fall, I became pregnant again, something Ivan and I both really wanted—another child to bring us joy and a sibling for Robert. In November, 1987, Mom, Dad, and Jay moved into their new apartment. After spending a day cleaning out cabinets and organizing the new apartment in preparation for their move, I noticed a bit of blood in my underpants, not a good sign. I visited my obstetrician who couldn't find our fetus' heartbeat. "I think you've had another miscarriage," he told me. I was heartbroken—I was already in love with this baby. The doctor sent me to an ultrasound lab to confirm what was going on. Fortunately, our baby was fine, which was an incredible relief. I had probably been a bit too ambitious with my cleaning and organizing and needed to take it a bit easier. I tried, although with a Type A personality, that was tough.

Three weeks before my due date, I developed a fever. After three days of an elevated temperature, my obstetrician was concerned enough to tell me to go to the hospital for tests. Ivan stayed at the hospital with me all day while various doctors and nurses came in and out of my room, taking blood, checking vitals, and asking questions. By 8 PM, the doctors were no closer to a diagnosis, but started me on intravenous antibiotics to combat a possible bacterial infection, such as listeria, which would be a significant danger to our baby. As Ivan was about to leave to get back home to take care of Robert, I said: "Maybe you'd better stay for a little while. I have some cramping and might be going into labor." An hour later, I was more certain that I was in labor and told the nurse that I needed to go to the labor room since I was having contractions.

Ivan had planned to watch the video I had purchased, a refresher Lamaze course, so he would know how to support me through my labor and delivery, but he was a bit of a procrastinator, to say the least, and had thought he had three more weeks to do so. I had watched the video and remembered that a tennis ball pushed against my lower back would help to reduce the severity of back labor pains, which I had experienced when I was in labor with Robert. A hospital is not the best place to find a tennis ball, however, so instead, Ivan jammed his fist into my lower back when I instructed him to. I asked the nurse to call my obstetrician who lived in Westchester County. Not having my prepared suitcase with me meant that I was missing the focal object that I had carefully chosen—an intricately decorated box. Since Ivan had a photo of Robert in his wallet, I suggested that as a substitute. I started using one of the lighter breathing techniques, while squinting at the tiny picture of Robert (I had taken off my eyeglasses that corrected for nearsightedness). I had decided to save the heavy-duty breathing methods for when the pain became more intense. I had already planned to get an epidural—I was not going to repeat the drug-free birth experience I had with Robert. One experience with unbearable pain was enough. When the nurse came into the room, I told her I was ready for drugs. "I'll check your progress." A moment later, she said, "It's too late for an epidural. You're ready to give birth. Let me find the doctor."

A resident walked in and said: "Your doctor is not here yet. Do you want to wait? Or do you want me to deliver your baby?" I didn't hesitate for even a second. I thought of what might have gone wrong when Mom was told to cross her legs since her doctor hadn't arrived yet when she was in labor with Ian. I didn't care if Ivan had to deliver our baby. I was not going to wait. "Go ahead. I'm ready." Ivan ran to put on surgical scrubs and barely made it into the delivery room since initially he was given two tops and no pants and had to scramble to find a full surgical outfit. Two pushes, and our daughter came into the world.

Elizabeth was born in June 1988, and in late July, we were ready to make our first trip with her, Robert, Mom, and Jay to BDC. The first part of the drive was fine that very hot day. But then the traffic came to a standstill. We turned on the radio to find out what was

     Harriet S. Mosatche

going on and soon learned that a water main had broken and that traffic wasn't moving—we had figured that last part out. I didn't panic at first. Elizabeth was asleep and Robert was talking to Ruthie (that's what he called my mother who loved the concept of being a grandmother but not the title). After being stopped for about an hour, we found a slow way off the highway. Unfortunately, love of my life, problem-solving Ivan then accidentally found a way back onto the same highway. That's when I panicked and screamed at him. Elizabeth was six weeks old. What if the air-conditioner stopped working? We were half-way between our house and BDC and had to decide whether we were going to return home or continue on. Part of my overly emotional reaction was probably due to the state of my postpartum hormones, but some of it was just my tendency toward expecting terrible things to happen. After three hours, we exited the highway onto city streets and finally to the parking lot of BDC. I was happy to see Ian who acted as if I were still pregnant, touching my stomach over and over while smiling. I explained that the baby Ivan was holding was Elizabeth and that I was no longer pregnant. Ian seemed so interested in the whole idea of pregnancy and babies that on subsequent visits, I developed a new game with him, pretending that he was pregnant by putting a doll or stuffed animal under his shirt, and then suddenly pulling it out with a loud congratulations. Ian laughed aloud when we did this. Or at least he did whenever he was not overly medicated into oblivion.

NO PROGRESS ON MOVING OUT OF BDC

Ian's annual report dated November 4, 1988 listed his progress on the goals that had been set for him, from "eating without spillage" (I would not do well on that goal as the many stains on my clothing can attest.) to "stacking shapes." What bothered me most about the report was the written comment at the end: "Ian's receptive language is at the 3-5 month age limit. His expressive language falls into the 2-3 month age level." I knew that wasn't accurate. He had a fairly extensive receptive language and could easily answer, using gestures or sounds, more than a hundred questions ranging from "What does a cardiologist take care of?" to "What kind of noise does an airplane make?" He could point to every part of his body and could even show the body part that was associated with a particular sensory function, such as "What do you smell with?" or "What do you hear with?" He aced them all.

Years earlier, I had repeatedly told BDC staff how Ian's abilities were underestimated. Since my explanations never led to more appropriate treatment, I eventually just stopped trying to get BDC staff to see Ian for what he was actually capable of, rather than what his official label ("profoundly retarded") said he should be. Typically I just read the reports quickly, became annoyed briefly, and then went on with the rest of my day. I had learned that focusing on what was written in those reports about Ian's abilities was not particularly relevant to the kind of care he received. Instead, we continued to advocate for specific actions that we knew would allow Ian to enjoy life a bit more—water play, rock and roll music, and verbal attention.

    Harriet S. Mosatche

By December 1988, fewer than 9,240 people remained residents in developmental centers in New York State. Unfortunately, Ian was still one of them. We weren't making any progress getting him out of BDC. Others were more successful, with 16,000 people with developmental disabilities living in community residences by the end of 1988. With two young children, part-time work, and helping out my parents, it was hard for me to find time to be an advocate for Ian. The best I could do for the next few years was to continue to make regular visits to BDC.

CHAPTER 16

Landmark Federal Legislation Passes While Ordinary Life Goes On

After suffering through three miscarriages and the stillbirth of a baby girl, Marsha gave birth to Ryan in February 1989, a wonderful addition to our family. Now, Ian had two nieces and two nephews. I hoped they would love him the way Marsha, Jay, and I did. I continued to include Robert and Elizabeth in our visits to BDC, and from time to time, Marsha and Steve also brought along Sherry and Ryan.

MORE CAUSE FOR CONCERN

Throughout 1989 and 1990, Ian's hospitalizations continued for a variety of reasons—sometimes there were incident reports, at other times nothing was written about the latest injury that required stitches or x-rays or the illness that had been neglected until it had reached a critical point. Each hospital visit was followed by a stay in the BDC infirmary. Although Ian was less likely to be hurt while he was there, he had absolutely nothing to do except lay in bed. I didn't know which was worse—a relatively safe environment but one totally devoid of stimulation or a setting that provided things to look at and do along with the strong possibility of injuries inflicted by other residents and staff.

From June 10 to June 22, 1990, Ian stayed at the hospital for treatment of cellulitis. Even though our family had informed staff at BDC that they had noticed swelling of his right knee, diagnosis and treatment with intravenous antibiotics were delayed for weeks. Hospital personnel indicated that Ian left the hospital in good condition on the 22nd, but he was back there that same day because of his obvious distress and swelling of his left leg. X-rays revealed a fracture of the proximal tibia, a bone in his leg. Ivan tried to uncover the cause of this significant injury—this was not just another abrasion or a black and blue mark—but each person blamed a different party. Hospital personnel assured us that Ian had to have been injured during the short time he was back at BDC, but staff at that institution said he must have been hurt while at the hospital. Ian's leg was put in a cast. For anyone, a cast is an annoyance. For Ian, a cast was torture. He kept asking me to remove it—by moving my hand over to his leg and looking up at me with eyes that begged me to make him more comfortable. Although I explained how it would help his leg heal, Ian couldn't understand why he had to have this heavy thing encasing his leg all day long. The cast also meant that he couldn't spend any time in the shower, which was one of his few pleasures at BDC.

In July of 1990, the Americans with Disabilities Act (ADA), modeled after the Civil Rights Act, was passed. This landmark federal legislation guaranteed people with disabilities the same rights in the workplace and public facilities as other citizens. I wondered whether there was any way that we could use this law to help Ian but knew it would take time for the ADA to make a tangible impact.

Ian remained in the BDC infirmary for four months until he was finally moved to a different wing. Although we expressed our opposition to this transfer because of the difficulty Ian had in adjusting to new people and environments, our opinions were ignored. Throughout the year Ian continued to suffer from bouts of cellulitis of his leg, a persistent fungal infection of his feet, bed sores, and ulcers. Ivan and I regularly suggested that these conditions persisted because Ian was allowed to sit for long periods with blood pooling in his feet, anti-fungal medication not applied regularly, and his diapers not changed frequently enough. Unfortunately, at that time other facilities that might have taken Ian were no better than BDC or were so far away that Ian would see us less often and we would be less effective advocates for what little humane care he received. Unless a placement was demonstrably superior, I saw no point in moving Ian. I felt trapped in a bad situation—doing whatever I could to help Ian but not succeeding in creating any real improvement in his living situation. My only glimmer of hope for Ian was that the new ADA legislation would eventually lead to better alternatives for him.

A GREAT LOSS

For years, I had confided in my cousin Myra who lived about a mile from my house. Often we played a Jane Fonda exercise video in what I called our "sunroom," a room that others might call a den, but one surrounded by windows and with two skylights. I told her about my visits with Ian, and how sad I was about how he lived and how frustrated I felt that I could not get him moved into a more suitable environment. She always listened sympathetically.

One afternoon when Myra came over to exercise, she told me that her doctor suggested that she undergo a few medical tests to find out why one of her glands was persistently swollen. Myra was only 45 and in great shape—it's probably nothing, I thought initially. But then I thought about all the things that went wrong in my family, and it hit me that it could be cancer. Whatever it was, I hoped it could be taken care of and Myra and I would go back to our mutual support system. Unfortunately, the diagnosis was lung cancer. My new role in Myra's life was to help her stay positive—through debilitating chemotherapy, hospital stays, and alternative therapies. Whenever she called me to come over because she was anxious or depressed, I changed my plans and went over there, often taking Elizabeth with me, and sometimes, Robert, too, when he wasn't in nursery school. Myra could no longer provide emotional support for me—her needs

     Harriet S. Mosatche

were too great, and I understood that. But it was hard not to have that person in my life whom I could tell everything to, who understood my concerns, particularly about Ian. On one of my visits, Myra said that she felt bad that everything was about her. She said: "As soon as I get better, I'm going to start being there for you." I told her not to worry, that I was glad that I could support her while she was ill. But the truth was that it was tough to give so much, when I was also giving to Ivan, my children, my parents, and Ian. I had my role to play, and I would play it—as well as I possibly could. And I did—right until the end when Myra died—a year and a half after her diagnosis.

Myra's death left a void in my life—she had been much more than a cousin to me. But I had to focus on the people who still needed me—particularly Ian. I was concerned about the sleeping medication Ian was routinely prescribed, with my cynical side believing that these were more for the convenience of the staff and less for Ian's welfare. In addition, he was still taking the anti-seizure medication Dilantin, and I worried about the long-term effects of that medication. As of September 1991, Ian had been seizure-free for five years, so it seemed to be time to evaluate how he would do with a decrease in dosage and maybe even weaning him off it. Instead the BDC team decided to keep Ian on the same level of medication and to observe him "for vomiting, diarrhea, blood dysersanis or hepatotoxicity as signs of Dilantin toxicity."

MORE MISINFORMATION

Ian's September 1991 report included the following sentences:

> *Ian's social interest seems to be concentrated in his being left alone. He prefers isolation to social interactive activities. Ian displays a limited interest in his environment, whether it be his immediate environment or outside surroundings. Ian's interest in music and visual events is minimal at best…Ian does not appear to enjoy most social activities and events. He is generally self-oriented.*

Where do I begin to disagree with all of this? Even a semi-conscious individual observing Ian with his family would recognize how enthusiastic and affectionate he was with us. It's true that when Ian was overmedicated he was not responsive. And when he was in a crowded room with a lot of loud, heavy metal music, he craved a quieter place. But when Ivan and I danced for and sometimes with Ian to an Elvis Presley record, he held his ears and grinned with obvious glee. And when he realized it was time for our visit to end (when we began to put our coats on), Ian asked for another story or song or more food, anything to keep us there a bit longer. Ian wanted company, but only if people knew what he liked to hear and do, and displayed genuine affection and praise for him. Like every other human. The staff report showed how little attention was paid to how Ian came alive when we visited and how little staff cared about modeling our behaviors.

Then there was the notation in the report that indicated that, "Mr. Rosenberg has no awareness of cause and effect at this time." The evidence to the contrary was obvious, and I didn't need my years of advanced training in developmental psychology to see it. Ian understood that pushing a light switch on created light in the room or putting his hand to his mouth led me to offer him water. Ian could find objects that I hid by figuring out their likely trajectory, such as a ball rolling behind a chair. But unless you made testing him fun, he was not going to cooperate. He followed my commands to "look under the blanket and give me the doll that is there" because he wanted to please me, but if a strange psychologist were to ask him to do the same task, he might not follow her request.

One sentence in that 1991 report captured staff's narrow and detrimental perceptions of Ian: "Ian continues to require frequent verbal and physical prompting and assistance for most gross motor tasks due to his lethargic and lazy nature." That statement demonstrated a total lack of understanding of how one's motivation to attend to a task is affected by an understanding of its purpose, and how lethargy is often a side effect of overmedication. The use of

     Harriet S. Mosatche

the word "lazy" reveals a startling ignorance of the nature of BDC's supposed mission and the people they were meant to help.

Over the years, Ian's reports never failed to mention his aggressiveness toward others. It was not until August 1992 that a staff member finally recognized that: "It is not clear whether these episodes are actually aggressive or just attempts to communicate. Staff have been instructed to use their judgment when filling out behavioral data sheets to distinguish between aggression and communication." That same report noted that Ian was motivated by "edibles and verbal praise." Finally, I saw an instance of common sense.

CHAPTER 17

Taking on Additional Responsibilities

When Elizabeth was four and Robert was six, I felt that the time was right for my return to full-time work. I had spent several years facilitating parenting workshops throughout the Bronx and Westchester County, teaching part-time at the College of New Rochelle, and doing freelance writing. Ivan was ready to give up his position as an associate in a New York City law firm where he never really felt comfortable (nothing like practicing law in Alaska) and was interested in starting his own practice closer to home. I returned to the Girl Scouts national office as the Director of Special Projects in September of 1992, and Ivan opened a law office in White Plains. Meanwhile the four of us visited Ian every other weekend. Both children understood that Ian was their uncle and my brother. They didn't complain about making the trip to Brooklyn since I made sure it was fun for them. We brought along toys, balls, books, and snacks for the visit and played traditional games such as Geography and 20 Questions during the car ride. My brother Jay taught us one game that became my favorite—Guess My Career. One person thought of a career, the more obscure and specific the better, and everyone else tried to guess by asking "yes" or "no" questions. Once Robert stumped us with his choice—a chinaware manufacturer. And no one was able to figure out Elizabeth's career of stunt double. The options were

 Harriet S. Mosatche

endless and often hilarious. And we continued to play that game on car trips for years.

ADVOCACY EFFORTS

Since Ivan was now self-employed, he took advantage of his flexible schedule to spend more time advocating for Ian to be moved to a group home within our county. He drafted letters for my parents to sign making official requests and also sought assistance from the Westchester Developmental Disabilities Services Office. Unfortunately, the letter we received on November 24, 1992 from the Disabilities office was not encouraging. It stated, in part:

> *My impression is that Mr. Rosenberg could be well served in a number of existing residences here in Westchester County. The problem is and will be the availability of a vacancy in one of those residences for him. At this point in time, we are not projecting any vacancies for the foreseeable future that would be appropriate for Mr. Rosenberg.*

By the end of 1992, Ian was 34, although he looked much younger. He always smiled when he saw Robert and Elizabeth, particularly when they sang or danced for him. I played a balancing act during those visits, making sure that Ian didn't get upset that I wasn't paying enough attention to him yet also helping my children see that they were always my first priority. But understanding that family members take care of each other was a lesson I hoped they would carry with them throughout their lives. At times, Elizabeth or Robert asked about what Ian understood or what he could do. They were impressed that he knew the answers to so many questions and sometimes added their own or suggested new ones for me to ask. Ian followed their every move. He laughed when they laughed. If they didn't think that Ivan or I were being careful enough with Ian, like maybe not cutting his sandwich into small enough pieces, one of them would ask: "Isn't that too big for him? He can choke on that."

Most of the time, the children were happy to be left alone (under our watchful eyes) to explore BDC's wide-open spaces indoors and out. They enjoyed the oversize barrels that they could turn when they ran inside them (basically hamster wheels for humans), the climbing equipment that was never used by any of the residents, and the basketball courts that were always available.

During one of our visits to BDC, we went over to the basketball courts to find the gates locked. When we inquired, an administrator told us that a group of prisoners was now housed in the building immediately next to the courts, and the courts were for their use only. The locks, we were told, were also to keep others safely away from the prisoners. Periodically, we checked the courts, both to see whether the gates were locked (maybe someone had reconsidered the practice) and whether the prisoners were actually using the courts. Yes, the gates continued to be locked, but we never saw anyone playing there.

Mom continued to join us on some of our visits to Ian, and as soon as he saw her, he touched his mouth, knowing that she always brought special treats for him, such as her homemade chocolate chip banana bread or butterscotch and chocolate cookies. Robert and Elizabeth loved having "our Ruthie" with them at "Ian's school." Calls of "Look at me" and "Watch this Ruthie" punctuated the quiet environment at BDC. Sometimes, Marsha and her family met us at BDC. Marsha's second child, her son Ryan, was just a little younger than Elizabeth and all four of the children would play together. Ian knew their names—always glancing at the child whose name had been called—and clapped his ears or smiled while watching their exploits. He put his hands out to catch the ball thrown to him and then passed it on to one of us. With so many family members present, we acted out "The Farmer in the Dell," with each of us playing a role and singing all stanzas. Ian happily complied with the request to pick a wife or a child or a dog. Whoever got picked would cheer, which pleased Ian, and the singing continued until the final "the cheese stands alone."

     Harriet S. Mosatche

CHANGES FOR MOM AND DAD

It was in 1993 that Mom and Dad were hospitalized on the same day. One winter weekday I stayed home from work since it was one of those teacher development days that made life very inconvenient for working parents. With Elizabeth attending a pre-school that didn't have the day off, it was an opportunity to spend time alone with Robert. While I was not the baking mom type, I asked Robert if he wanted to make chocolate chip cookies that winter afternoon. Soon after we had slipped the cookie trays on the oven racks and set the timer, the phone rang. It was Mom. "You need to come over here right away," she said in a strangely frightened voice. "You have to take me out of this place. I want to go home." I didn't understand what she was talking about or where she could be.

"But you are home," I insisted, believing that logic would prevail. How was I so sure that Mom was home? Because for many years, my mother never left the house unaccompanied—an agoraphobic years before it became a widely recognized diagnosis—terrified that she would forget who she was or that she would have a heart attack.

"No, I'm not. I'm in that place Ivan took me to once before, and I don't want to be here. Please take me out of here." My heart started to race—had Mom had a stroke?

I tried reassuring my mom. "Now, I want you to hang up the phone. I'm going to call your home number, and you'll see that the phone will ring and you'll pick it up." So we both hung up and I quickly dialed the number, as I calmly explained to Robert that Ruthie needed me to call her back. I must be an incredibly stupid optimist, but I actually believed that when I called my parents' home phone number, Mom would have just snapped out of it—whatever "it" was. And dear, sweet, loving normal Mom would be back. But when Mom answered the phone, she was as confused as before, insisting that she was not at home. "But I just called your home phone number. You must be home," I explained, trying to will her into understanding the reality of the situation. My usually agreeable mother just kept saying that I had to get her out of there.

A phone call to Ivan, a call to her doctor, a trip to the hospital, a CAT scan, an MRI and other tests, and before the day was over, I was told that Mom probably had Alzheimer's. "That couldn't be," I said to the doctor. "It wouldn't show up so suddenly."

"That's true," he agreed. But then he asked me to try to remember other signs. Yes, there were the two occasions when Mom found herself outside her apartment in the middle of the night wearing her nightgown. But when she had laughed off these incidents, I did, too. I wasn't ready to give in yet, to accept this horrible diagnosis. The doctor wasn't really sure, I said to myself. He doesn't know Mom. It's her anxiety that has gotten to her. Or maybe it's a mild stroke that just didn't show up on the CAT scan or the MRI. Anything but Alzheimer's, the disease that would rob Mom of her personality.

It took a while for me to accept the diagnosis. Me—the psychologist, the former professor who knew all the signs and symptoms of this disease. But it's so different when it's your mother. Why did it have to happen to her—to this generous and kind person who had already given so much of her life to taking care of Ian? Grandma would have said that it was God's will. I wish I could be religious enough to believe that. All I knew was that Elizabeth and Robert were going to lose the Ruthie they adored, and I was going to lose my best friend.

Of course, we were Rosenbergs, and the day was not over yet. Ivan had brought Dad to our house and then went back to stay with Mom at the hospital. I was clearing the dishes after dinner when Dad slipped from his chair to the floor unconscious. An ambulance took Dad to the hospital—he had suffered a mild stroke. Mom and Dad became roommates at the hospital, while we tried to figure out with Marsha and her husband Steve what to do next. Mom had been taking care of Dad who had been suffering for years with severe arthritis. Complications of his knee replacement surgery years earlier had resulted in a severe infection and the loss of his short-term memory. He couldn't take care of himself, let alone prevent Mom from doing something dangerous. Although Jay was living

     Harriet S. Mosatche

with them, his long-term depression, anxiety, and OCD didn't make him a viable candidate to be a full-time caretaker for both parents. And Jay would not tolerate any aides living with them, even if there were room in their apartment.

For a brief moment, I thought about the possibility of moving my parents into our house and arranging for an aide to care for them while Ivan and I were at work. But I wanted my children to have a happier childhood than what would have been possible with my parents requiring constant attention. We were already spending lots of time visiting or calling about Ian and taking my parents to doctors. I didn't think we should take on any more. Part of my decision was selfish. If my parents were to live with us, I would be giving up all means of escape from the family problems that had burdened me almost my entire life. I had seen the resentment my mother felt toward my grandmother as she became more of a burden. Both of my parents needed 24/7 assistance—I admit I was not willing to give that to them, no matter how much I loved them.

After several weeks in the hospital, where we visited them often, Mom and Dad moved into a nursing home in White Plains near Ivan's office. Mom's condition deteriorated quickly. She was assaulted and knocked to the floor by her roommate (also suffering from dementia) just a few days after arriving. The result was a fractured hip that required surgery and rehabilitation. I spent a lot of time with Mom in the hospital, encouraging her to do the physical therapy that might allow her to walk again. Shortly after returning to the nursing home, Mom fell out of bed during the night and her leg began to swell. She returned to the hospital, and an orthopedic surgeon said she needed surgery immediately to reduce the swelling or she might develop gangrene. In the meantime, Ivan, who had become an advocate not just for Ian but for everyone in the family, asked for a neurological consult since Mom might have hit her head in the fall. When Ivan told the neurologist that the orthopedist planned to operate, the neurologist said, "He can't do that. She'll bleed to death on the operating table. Her blood tests show that she's very low on clotting factors."

Ivan relayed that information to the orthopedist and asked why he hadn't considered that. "I'm just a carpenter," was his response. "The doctor needs to look into that." Oh, so the orthopedic surgeon doesn't think he's a doctor? Very interesting. And scary. Ivan then "fired" that surgeon and brought someone else in, who understood that considering the whole person was important in medicine.

Mom's physical condition gradually improved, but she never walked again. Her kidneys soon began to fail after years of worsening kidney function. She needed dialysis, which the hospital's doctor advised us against. "What kind of life does she have now with her dementia?" he asked Marsha and me. "Let her die." How dare he suggest that? What kind of physician tries to persuade children to give up on their mother? And in such an uncaring way? She still recognized all of us, made jokes from time to time, and was not in pain. I asked her whether she wanted dialysis, and she said "yes." She was not ready to give up, even though she was confused much of the time.

THE NEW NORMAL

Our weekend schedule was now really packed—visiting Ian every other weekend in Brooklyn, seeing my parents every weekend in White Plains, accompanying Robert to his soccer or hockey games all over the New York metropolitan area, driving Liz to her dance lessons, and taking care of all the ordinary stuff like grocery shopping and gardening. Fortunately, the nursing home arranged for transportation for Mom's dialysis sessions three times a week. During the week, Ivan checked in on my parents whenever he could. Just as he had been doing with Ian for years, Ivan became my parents' advocates. He loved them—in some ways more than his own parents, he told me often—and wanted them well-taken care of. Unlike Mom's worsening condition, Dad seemed to flourish in the nursing home with regular meals, attention from staff, and visits from my family and Marsha's. A few other people stopped by occasionally, including Ivan's mother as well as Dad's brother Hy

     Harriet S. Mosatche

and sister-in-law Frances. I told my parents that we were trying to get Ian moved into a group home near where they now lived so he could visit them. I didn't talk to Ian about Mom and Dad, thinking it would be too painful for him to hear about them but not see them.

CHAPTER 18

A New Role for Ivan and a Loss for All of Us

After so many years of frustration reading Ian's reports, those from 1993 finally showed a different tone. He was no longer said to be lethargic and lazy, self-centered and aggressive. Rather he was described in July 1993 as "rather active and happy when engaged in acts where attention is given to him. He enjoys one-on-one attention from staff." It had taken decades for staff to arrive at that realization. Or more likely, it was the infusion of recently trained staff who had a greater understanding of the needs and characteristics of the residents. It was probably not a coincidence that a year had gone by since Ian had paid a visit to the hospital emergency room. Unlike previous reports that indicated that he was indifferent to music, this one said that he "continues to enjoy listening to music. He seems to enjoy storytelling and puppet play." One staff member even noted that "Ian will try to propel his wheelchair closer to staff when interacting" with them. For the first time, I saw a section on the annual report labeled "Strengths." This focus was consistent with the latest thinking in the field of youth development, the area in which I was employed. Instead of viewing individuals in terms of their deficits, youth workers were encouraged to look for strengths and assets. Maybe, at last, the passage of the ADA was beginning to have an impact.

IVAN'S ADVOCACY ACTIONS

After attending a meeting of GROW, an advocacy organization in New York launched and run by parents of people with developmental disabilities, Ivan decided to volunteer as an ombudsperson at a local group home. While doing something worthwhile for people who could use an objective advocate, he would make connections that might ultimately help us get Ian into a similar facility. Ivan went through the required training and started making official visits to his assigned group home. The residents were high-functioning females, largely young adults who lit up when Ivan visited. He listened to their stories and complaints, and then followed up with recommendations about actions that could make the group home function even better. Mostly, he felt that his presence was a reminder to staff that someone was checking up on them. To the women who lived there, he was a man who cared about their welfare. When Ivan brought our children Elizabeth and Robert to visit, the residents were thrilled. The one time I accompanied Ivan to the women's home, they were not very friendly to me, but they treated him as if he were Prince Charming. Realizing that I was a threat to the fantasies they had obviously created, I stayed away after that. But the visit gave me a vision of what kind of home Ian might live in one day.

While we and many other families were trying to pressure New York State to make group homes in the community available to those with developmental disabilities, many members of the general public made known their negative views of community placement through protests and court cases. Even when not stated in such blunt terms, the basic idea behind the objections was "Not In My Backyard." When interviewed by television broadcasters, protesters said things like: "I have nothing against people who are mentally retarded. But we already have one group home in this area." Or someone would couch their objections in terms that indicated that their concern was for the residents, saying: "The house being considered is on a very busy street. Mentally retarded people would not be safe with all that traffic." What they were really saying was: "I don't want people with mental retardation living where I can see them." Or, "Having them in my neighborhood will hurt property values." Or, "They're dangerous and I'm afraid they'll hurt my children." Yes, those with severe cognitive disabilities need supervision both to keep them and their neighbors safe, but they are as entitled to live in the community as everyone else. It was 1994, and progress to help people like Ian was achingly slow. Is it only those with siblings and children who have disabilities who could understand that?

Thankfully, Ivan has never been one to give up easily. Throughout 1994 and 1995, he bombarded Westchester County officials with letters, reports, and phone calls about Ian. In a letter from April 1994 to the county's Department of Community Mental Health, Ivan wrote that: "…Both of Ian's parents, who are in their mid to late 70's are now wheelchair-bound, and Mrs. Rosenberg is on kidney dialysis two to three times a week. Because of their medical conditions, neither has been able to see Ian in over a year… As a practical matter unless Ian is moved to Westchester, he will not be able to see his parents before they die."

Aside from inexplicably referring to Ian as "James" (the one and only time a name was used) in his lengthy annual report from BDC written in June 1994, everything remained status quo. Goals continued to focus on Ian washing his hands, brushing his teeth, and feeding himself—all activities he had been able to do for years. The report included numerous descriptions of abrasions treated with Bacitracin, treatment for athlete's foot, and recurrent cellulitis of both his legs and his face. He had lost 12 pounds but was said to have a good appetite and to eat well. Ever since Ian had arrived at BDC, he was described as functioning at the lowest cognitive level— profound retardation. While I had explained to staff on numerous occasions why that label underestimated his abilities, it was never changed. The description began to seem more problematic to me as time went on because it might prevent Ian from being placed in a group home. So Ivan and I sought to get Ian's level changed

   Harriet S. Mosatche

from profoundly to severely mentally retarded. At least staff now routinely recognized that when Ian pinched or grabbed people, it was not done to hurt them but rather to get their attention or to express his frustration since he could not express himself verbally.

An October 1994 letter from Ivan to the Director of the Westchester Developmental Disabilities Service Office included Ian's annual report and explained why Ian's inability to walk or use the toilet were a function of having been beaten and the lack of proper care at BDC. Ivan also wrote that: "…As a participant in the Westchester County Volunteer Ombudsman Program for over a year, I have observed that the group homes offer far more opportunities for activities and stimulation than BDC. I sincerely hope that you are able to open a group home to which Ian can be transferred in the near future."

TOO LATE FOR MOM

By September 1995, Mom had not seen Ian in almost three years. By that time, she no longer recognized me, but she never failed to respond with "I love you, too, darling" whenever I told her I loved her. I could still make her smile, but she was getting weaker. Marsha and I had both been thinking that perhaps it was time to institute a Do Not Resuscitate (DNR) order for Mom. We were definitely not ready when the doctor had suggested it a couple of years earlier when Mom's Alzheimer's and kidney disease were far less advanced. Now, she was spending more time in the hospital than anywhere else, and the quality of her life had deteriorated markedly in the past year. At 11 PM on September 16th, a doctor from White Plains Hospital called to say that Mom was bleeding internally and strongly suggested that I might want a DNR order to be put in place. As Mom's health proxy, I agreed. Ivan asked if I wanted to go the hospital that night. "No" I responded. "We can go tomorrow. Let's let the children sleep." We had made that trip to the emergency room to see Mom many times over the past couple of years. At 6 AM on September 17th, Ivan answered the phone. He turned to me and gently said, "She's gone." Ivan called Marsha, and I broke the sad news to my children. Then I cried—not because my mother had died. I cried because I realized that I would never be able to have another conversation with my real mother, the pre-Alzheimer's one. And we had not been able to move Ian to Westchester in time for him to see his mother one more time.

After a week of sitting shiva for Mom (a time for others to visit after a loved one's death—a ritual practiced by Jewish people), I went back to work. Marsha, Jay, and I talked about whether we would tell Ian and decided against it. Since we didn't know how much Ian understood about death, how could he possibly benefit from learning that Mom was gone? He couldn't speak about his grief, and therefore we would be at a loss in terms of when and how to comfort him.

SEEKING HELP FOR MYSELF

While Mom's death was not unexpected, I had a hard time dealing with this loss. Probably because the loss was on top of a life that was already feeling overwhelming, I began to feel anxious. It wasn't to the extent that I couldn't go to work or take care of my children or talk to Ivan or my friends, but just enough anxiety to make me feel that if my emotional state deteriorated further, I might develop an anxiety disorder like the one that had plagued Mom throughout her adult life. I understood intellectually that my anxiety was not rational, but I couldn't will myself out of those feelings just because I knew they didn't make sense. Deciding to see a psychologist was not an easy decision for me, even though I had a Ph.D. in the field and knew that research supported its efficacy. I saw myself as strong and confident. Why couldn't I just deal with the latest crisis without professional help?

Once I actually started seeing a therapist, I understood its appeal. In everyday life, I was typically the one who made others feel comfortable, offered advice, asked questions, and initiated problem-solving. But in this setting, all I had to do was talk about

     Harriet S. Mosatche

myself and my issues, and not be concerned about how someone else might react to what I was saying or the emotions I was expressing. Of course, I talked about Ian. His existence had a greater impact on the arc of my life than anyone or anything else. His "fingerprints" could be found in every part of my life. I judged people by how they treated him. I chose my profession because of him. I made career decisions based, at least in part, on his needs. I became more accepting of others who were different because he helped me understand how similar we all are.

In one of my therapy sessions, I explained to Dr. F that while Ivan was not particularly romantic nor as attentive as I would have liked, he was incredible with Ian. Ivan never complained about the hours spent in traffic on the way to and from Brooklyn to visit Ian twice a month. As Ian's main advocate, Ivan called BDC and hospital administrators, wrote letters on Ian's behalf, and represented Ian's interests in meetings. I was so grateful for all the time Ivan spent trying to improve Ian's life that I had to overlook what my husband didn't do for me. Until Dr. F asked me: "What about for you? What you've described are all the ways Ivan has been a wonderful brother-in-law. You should expect your husband to also do things directly for you." I listened to what Dr. F said, and part of me recognized that she had made a point that I hadn't wanted to admit, even to myself. But it was true that I was so grateful to Ivan for his advocacy and actions on Ian's behalf that I accepted being shortchanged by Ivan in terms of attention and affection. I didn't continue therapy for very long, not because that conversation hadn't touched a chord—it most certainly had—but it was one of the very few insights Dr. F had. She never took notes and didn't seem to remember most of what I had told her just a week before. After Dr. F referred me to a psychiatrist who prescribed medication to treat my anxiety, I decided I could find other uses for the time and money I was spending on my therapy.

CHAPTER 19

Growing Up with Uncle Ian

As tweens, my children were busy with school, piano lessons, and friends, and Ivan and I were eager spectators at Robert's ice hockey and soccer games and at Elizabeth's dance lessons and recitals. But one or both of them usually accompanied us when we made our trek to BDC. Our supplies included balls, snacks, drinks, playing cards, and books—we could easily have been away for a couple of days. Once in a while Elizabeth or Robert made plans with friends that coincided with a scheduled visit to Ian. I did not want them to feel obligated to join us, so most of the time when one of them asked, I freely gave permission for them to spend time with peers. Other times, they chose not to go on a play date and would tell their friends, "I'm going to visit my Uncle Ian today. He lives in Brooklyn." Ian was a huge and important part of our lives, but I wanted my children to have a fun childhood that was not overly focused on Ian's welfare. I didn't want them to feel burdened the way I had when I was growing up, and still felt from time to time when so much of a weekend was spent on a visit to Ian. I loved him deeply and couldn't imagine life without him, but sometimes, I thought about what my life would have been like if he hadn't been born. I felt guilty about those thoughts. How selfish they seemed—particularly since Ian showed his love for me in the most unconditional way. It didn't matter how I looked or whether I had brought anything for him—he showed his appreciation for my visit by touching my arm gently, grinning at me with his mouth and his eyes, and laughing at my stories. He noticed everything about me. Ian touched his hair when I got a haircut, and he pointed to his eyes when I wore new eyeglasses. Ivan remarked that he needed Ian to clue him in to those changes since Ian was often more attentive to such details than my husband.

DANGERS IN AND AROUND BDC

I never let up my guard about the dangers in and around the grounds of BDC. While I didn't want to frighten our children, I reminded them to keep their distance from Ian and the other residents. I knew how to avoid Ian when he tried to grab me, but it took years before I felt comfortable allowing Elizabeth, who was so petite, to stand within touching distance of him. Never forgetting how other residents had severely injured Ian, I wanted all of us to be prepared to prevent a kick, bite, or pinch from those who had no other means of communication. I showed Robert and Elizabeth how you could be friendly with the residents of BDC while not getting too close—at least until we knew who was likely to reach out to grab a visitor and who was more passive. I felt guilty about teaching my children the choreography of avoiding residents who approached them physically. But I'm always a mother first.

Condoms and syringes often littered the BDC parking lot. I could only imagine the partying there on Saturday night—definitely not by the residents of BDC but by those who lived in the neighborhood. After we parked the car, I warned Robert and Elizabeth to watch where they stepped and not to dare touch anything on the ground. We would hurry inside the main building and find a table or bench to set up our stuff while Ivan headed to Ian's residential wing to bring him down. Whenever Ivan took longer than usual to meet us, my thoughts turned to the myriad things that could have gone wrong. What a relief to see Ian's smile as Ivan wheeled him toward us. Elizabeth once told me that she wondered why we didn't take her to see Ian's room. She assumed it was because we were afraid for her safety. The real reason, however, was my anxiety about the condition we would find Ian in. Since Ivan had no such issue, his job was to pick up Ian from his wing, inquire about any new bruises, and bring him to the main building area where we were waiting.

SPECIAL ACTIVITIES FOR MY CHILDREN AND IAN

In spite of my apprehensions about our visits to BDC, Elizabeth has fond and very distinct memories of learning to use a swing at BDC. At a park near our house, she would have been embarrassed to have her dad teach her the proper technique, but at BDC, she didn't care what the staff and residents thought of an 8 year-old learning a skill she probably should have mastered years earlier. As Elizabeth remembers it, "Dad told me to imagine that there was a bar in front of me and I had to swing my legs over it. Then once I did that it would be released and I had to hold it tight with my legs until I got all the way to the back again and then let it go so it would drop."

During the winter when we couldn't take Ian outside because we never could get him to keep his jacket sleeves below his elbow or keep a hat and gloves on, we set up our stuff in one of the "private" brightly colored corridors of the main building—the places rarely used by others. Robert and Elizabeth were content to play card games, such as War or Uno, or more often run around without an adult telling them to slow down or stop. Their laughter echoed in the hallways, such a contrast to the dismal conditions we often encountered.

The children often brought a soccer ball with them, and BDC was the one place we allowed them to play with it indoors. But when the weather wasn't too cold for Ian's uncovered hands and head, they practiced their skills in the many accessible outdoor areas. Robert never seemed to tire of kicking a soccer ball against the concrete blocks of the building walls. We always brought snacks for Ian and the children, but I never ate while I was at BDC. Being there caused me to lose my appetite, even for my favorite foods. If someone

     Harriet S. Mosatche

had offered me lobster drizzled with hot butter sauce followed by a Linzer tart, I could easily have declined. If I had stayed at BDC for several weeks, I would most certainly have lost all the weight I had gained during my pregnancies, lots of extra pounds that have stuck to me to this day.

When we picked up Jay to join us on our visits, he often had a gift for our children. One Easter, Jay gave Elizabeth a chocolate bunny and said it was from him and Ian. Jay often signed his cards to us, "Love, Ian and Jay." Ian was always named first. Sometimes, Jay signed cards to one of us as simply, "Love, Ian" and the sentiments were expressed as Ian's. A card to Ivan "signed" by Ian might say, "I love it when you tell me the Willie Dreshen story and often wonder whatever happened to that man." Jay had his own mental health problems to deal with so our family was especially grateful for his sweetness in speaking for Ian through cards and gifts.

Although most people don't particularly relish oral exams, Ian loved being tested, partly, I speculated, because of our cheers when he showed us what he knew, and partly because it was an opportunity for him to feel competent. It was a way to keep Ian engaged and learning. I was typically the questioner, although as Elizabeth got older, she asked to take on the role or would think of new questions we could ask Ian. She said that it was boring for him to keep getting the same questions and that we should be trying to teach him new things. I had fallen into the trap of focusing on what Ian couldn't do rather what he was capable of learning. Elizabeth reminded me that we should be putting more effort into exposing Ian to new information just as we did with her. And lo and behold, in spite of BDC's assessment, Ian learned new concepts and had fun in the process.

To make things more interesting for Ian—and me—I divided his questions into categories with some having more point values than others. While Body Part questions (such as "Where is your hand?" or "Point to your head") were only worth one point each, Functional questions (such as "What do you think with?" or "You touch with your _____?") counted for two points each. Medical Specialties included items about what cardiologists and psychiatrists do. I even created a Disabilities category, which allowed Ian to tell us what people who were deaf, blind, or crippled couldn't do, with each item worth three points. More politically correct terms, such as motor impairment, were not yet part of the language used to discuss disabilities, and could have been too abstract for Ian to understand. Then there was the Miscellaneous category, with questions I added such as, "What does an electroencephalogram measure?" When Elizabeth saw Ian point to his head in response, she asked what an electroencephalogram was, impressed that Ian knew something she didn't. He had experienced the test that included measuring brain waves in one of his many evaluations and remembered what it was called. At the age of 11, Elizabeth began wearing braces on her teeth and said it was time to teach Ian about the job of an orthodontist. Ian already knew that dentists worked on people's teeth and that Dad's friend Irving Goldschein was a dentist, but orthodontist was a new career for Ian. Pointing to his teeth when asked what an orthodontist did became part of Ian's repertoire. At the end of the test, I gave Ian his score, and everyone cheered for him. Ian joined in, rubbing his ears and grinning, clearly proud of his accomplishment.

Even when we had a really good visit with Ian, I still found it hard to leave him, knowing that we would not be back for two weeks and wondering what might happen to him during our absence. When our children were with us, I worked hard to make the car rides as pleasant as possible. But we were often stuck in traffic, and what should have been an hour drive each way often turned into 90 minutes or more. To alleviate her boredom during those endless drives, Elizabeth sometimes tried to draw or read, but nausea quickly put a stop to those activities. More successful were singing, playing car games, and pointing out special sites, such as The New York Times building, the Unisphere left over from the 1964 World's Fair in Queens, and the never-ending construction of the railroad to the JFK airport. Often, as we passed each place, I related stories of how it figured in my childhood, like describing those wondrous visits to the World's Fair where we could see what the future might look like with electric cars and multiple function kitchen appliances. Or how Jay got hurt on a ride because he wasn't properly secured by restraints.

A NEW BOOK AND A NEW POSSIBILITY FOR IAN

Ian continued to live at BDC, and once a year, we received a Comprehensive Functional Assessment for Ian with sections, categories, and rating scales probably mandated by government regulations. Most of the report consisted of the description of irrelevant minutiae, such as this description in the Sexuality section: "He has no knowledge, nor comprehension of sexuality, precautionary measures, STDs or birth control methods, condoms, etc. He is currently not sexually active." A simple Not Applicable would have sufficed for that section.

In a typical thirty-page report, here and there were comments worth reading. In 1996, at the age of 37, Ian was said to be "mischievous and playful—he likes being touched by appropriate persons, and he likes to reach out and touch and interact with staff (sometimes you can hardly get away from him)." A section titled "Awareness of Cause and Effect" contained the following: "Mr. Rosenberg can push a button to activate a switch. He smiles and laughs when he sees the results of his actions." For so many years, the only comments had been negative and focused on what Ian couldn't do. It was a pleasure to read those sentences that described Ian's skills.

On August 19, 1998, New York Governor George Pataki announced a five-year plan to eliminate the waiting list for residential services for those individuals considered to have developmental disabilities or mental retardation. The NYS-CARES plan, which stood for New York State Creating Alternatives in Residential Environments and Services, gave us hope for the first time since Ian's childhood that he might be able to live again in a home environment.

By 1999, Robert had started high school and Elizabeth was a middle school student. My second book was about to be published, one that I had started working on when Robert was in middle school when I couldn't find an appropriate guidebook for boys his age. Many years had elapsed since the publication of my first book, and it was exciting to promote *Too Old for This, Too Young for That! Your Survival Guide for the Middle School Years.* Although the book contained information about sibling relationships, it didn't include anything about dealing with those with severe disabilities, although I knew that I was not the only sibling who grew up in that situation.

          Harriet S. Mosatche

CHAPTER 20

Changes in the Air

The climate was beginning to change, not just in the state of New York, but also across the country regarding the perception and treatment of people with disabilities. The public and the government seemed more interested in their welfare and education. In the 1999 case of Olmstead v. L.C., the U. S. Supreme Court decided that public agencies must offer services to individuals with mental disabilities in the most integrated setting possible. Even as I applauded these advances, I was growing more and more discouraged by our lack of progress in moving Ian out of BDC.

MORE OF THE SAME

Ian's July 1999 annual report included a long list of bodily injuries he had suffered during the year, including numerous scratch marks on his left upper arm, abrasions on his legs and elbows, facial cuts near his eyes, swelling and redness of his lower and upper back, and a swollen toe that required splinting. When we questioned staff about these injuries as they occurred, they invariably said they were self-inflicted. Ian couldn't even reach parts of his back that were red and swollen. It was obvious to me that labeling the source as "self-abuse" was an ideal excuse since Ian was unable to refute those claims.

In the psychological assessment section of the report, Ian was described in the following way:

> *His affect is flat, although at times he displays different
> emotions such as laughing or smiling…Mr. Rosenberg
> also has a history of feces smearing. This behavior occurs
> infrequently and if he is supervised closely, it will not occur.*

I knew that Ian's affect was *not* flat. When he was happy, he smiled. When something funny happened, he laughed. When he enjoyed a song, he rubbed his ears and head. When he was upset, he grimaced or grunted. When he was frustrated, he growled. When he was sad or in pain, he cried. Observing one visit with his family would have shown the writers of that report a great range of emotional response. Then there was the part about the feces smearing, something I had seen on previous reports. What I wondered was: If this behavior does not occur when he is supervised closely, then why isn't that being done?

AN IN-PERSON REQUEST AND A RAY OF HOPE

In October 1999, I learned that New York's Governor Pataki was going to visit the synagogue we belonged to during a Hanukkah celebration. Although I rarely attended services at Beth-El and was a lifelong Democrat, I planned to attend the event where the Republican governor was scheduled to speak. I couldn't miss an opportunity to raise a question about the implementation of NYS-CARES. After Governor Pataki's short upbeat presentation, he stayed to accept well wishes from enthusiastic congregants. I wiggled my way through the crowd to reach out to shake the governor's hand, quickly saying: "I have a problem I need your help with. My brother is mentally retarded and has been living in the Brooklyn Developmental Center for 25 years. He has been on a waiting list to get into a group home for a decade, and nothing has happened yet. As our governor, you have a responsibility to all your citizens."

The governor, seemingly flustered by my direct request, grabbed one of his assistants and said to him "Give her your business card." To me, he said, "He'll help you," and then strode quickly out of the room.

            Harriet S. Mosatche

While I was trying to influence an elected official in my direct and personal way, Ivan was busy writing letters, including one on December 8, 1999 to the Westchester Department of Mental Health. Ivan included Ian's most recent quarterly report and corrected one important piece of information in that report. He wrote:

> *Under "Level of Contact," the report indicates that there were no visits in the quarter. That comment is incorrect, and I have brought it to the attention of MW (name of a staff member). My wife and I visit Ian generally every other weekend… Apparently, whoever checked the visitor's log (which I religiously sign each time we visit Ian) could not find the log for Ian or looked only at the first page, which happens to be blank.*

Ivan went on to inquire about the current status of planning for new barrier-free group homes in Westchester County and noted that he had not heard back from any agency that might have a group home vacancy appropriate for Ian.

Shortly after that letter was mailed, Ivan received a phone call from Jane, the Director of Quality Management and Training at Richmond Children's Center. She said she had visited Ian at BDC and would like to meet us to discuss the possibility of placing him in a new group home in Yonkers that her agency was going to open up in a few months. I told myself not to get too excited—we didn't yet know whether Ian would be accepted—but this was the closest we had ever gotten to moving Ian out of BDC.

REAL PROGRESS

In late December 1999, we arranged to meet with Jane at an existing group home. Unfortunately, there were no vacancies there, but we were assured that a group home opening in Yonkers would be very similar. Ivan and I walked to the front door of a real house—nothing set it apart as a setting for those who had disabilities, except for the ramp leading to the front door. It turned out that we had passed that house many times since it was close to the middle school Elizabeth was attending. Like the exterior, the house's interior did not look institutional in any way. The residents who were home seemed clean, comfortable, and happy. The home was bright and inviting—immediately inside we saw a dining room table, a couch, rugs, and pictures on the walls. Ian could flourish in a place like that. I told Jane how much I wanted this kind of environment for my brother and how appreciative I was that this dream might become a reality soon.

Ivan completed the necessary paperwork to get Ian transferred to a Westchester County group home, and I signed a Memorandum of Understanding NYS-CARES Assurances, laying out my understanding as well as Richmond's of the details of our agreement. For me, the most important line was: "Richmond Children's Center, Inc. has discussed with Ian Rosenberg and his sister the following residential options: A six-person IRA." I quickly learned that the kind of IRA referred to in this document had nothing to do with saving for retirement; rather it stood for Individualized Residential Alternative.

On January 18, 2000, a social worker from Richmond completed a detailed individualized service plan for Ian. With a report that starts with, "Ian is a very special adult who is 41 years old..." I could already feel the difference in attitude between Ian's current and hopefully future environment. The report also described BDC in the following way:

> *The Center is very institutional in nature and consists of four residential buildings, along with one main building...Ian shares a room with another resident in a small, confined area. Ian is not stimulated enough at Brooklyn Developmental Center, since there is limited programming offered to him... Staff hardly engage with Ian so he then appears to be stoic and inactive. He is not stimulated to his maximum potential.*

     Harriet S. Mosatche

Ian's final Annual Summary report at BDC was dated May 9, 2000. Yes, at last our efforts had paid off—this was the last time Ian would be evaluated as a BDC resident. The only relevant part of the 33-page report was the phrase, "accepted on 3/31/00," referring to his placement by the Richmond Children's Center agency. The move was official—only the date remained in question. The house in Yonkers—River House—that was to become Ian's home had to be upgraded with safety items, such as automatic sprinklers and smoke alarms, with a new kitchen, and with sturdy furniture. All six residents would move in during the same time period. Like Ian, a few were moving from institutional settings. But a couple were being placed outside their family home for the first time.

For everyone, it would be an adjustment. But the house was located just a 10-minute drive from our house, which made it convenient for us to visit. And Jay's apartment—my parents' old place—was about a mile away, and I knew Jay would visit often. My one concern was about Ian's roommate. How would he react when Ian woke him up at night? What would he do when Ian reached out to him? I kept thinking about how much Ian had suffered at the hands of Bill, Ian's first roommate at BDC, the young man who had seemed so friendly when we met him. But for now, I tried to push aside the worries and feel the joy of Ian living in a real home close to our family.

LEARNING ABOUT RICHMOND COMMUNITY SERVICES

Now that I knew that Ian would be moving to River House, I grew impatient. I wanted it to happen immediately. On May 31, I signed four forms, authorizing the release of information from BDC and other agencies that would allow Ian to receive a variety of services, including an enrichment day program run by Richmond Community Services. Two weeks later, I was still waiting for the day of Ian's move. BDC requested that before Ian could move, he needed to make a "pre-placement visit" to the proposed new residence. On June 13th, Ivan and I composed a letter requesting that the requirement be waived. Our letter stated, in part:

As you know, Ian is non-verbal and is severely retarded. Thus, he would not be able to communicate his impressions of the River House facility to anyone. It is possible that he could be excited about seeing a new place and new faces, or he could be frightened. We cannot predict his reaction. His immediate reaction would not be relevant in any event to a decision on placement.

The truth was that I was concerned that if Ian grabbed a staff member or growled in a way that might seem threatening because he was either excited or frightened, Richmond Community Services might rescind their invitation and close down the possibility of his living in a real home once again. Our letter to BDC went on to say:

There is an additional reason for expediting Ian's move to Yonkers. Ian's father is in a nursing home in White Plains, and he is not in good health. Ian has not seen his father in over ten years because it was not feasible to transport either one of them between Westchester County and Brooklyn to see each other since both of them are non-ambulatory. We would like to make sure that Ian and his father can see each other before his father dies. Once Ian has moved to Yonkers, we plan to transport him to his father's nursing home in White Plains, so the two of them can see each other again.

In researching the background of the agency sponsoring the group home where Ian was going to live, I learned that a woman named Ellen Richmond brought a baby with evident cognitive impairment into her home in 1938 after the child had been born at Mt. Vernon Hospital. That act of humanity led to the creation of the Richmond Sanitarium, which closed in 1973, followed by the opening of the Richmond Children's Center in Yonkers, New York. Unlike large state institutions like BDC, Richmond prided itself on its "warm, loving environment." It was bittersweet to know that such a place

     Harriet S. Mosatche

existed and that Ian was finally moving there, but that we hadn't discovered it in 1988 when my parents moved from Brooklyn to Westchester County.

CHAPTER 21

A New Home for Ian, Finally

L ots of people view the number 13 as unlucky. But it was on the 13th day of July 2000 that Ian at age 41 moved from Brooklyn into his new home in Yonkers. It was hard for me to concentrate at work that day. I couldn't wait to see him in his group home. Although Robert and Elizabeth wanted to join us, I was concerned that Ian would become overstimulated by a lot of company, so just Ivan and I planned to visit that first day. Unlike the typical 60 to 90 minute drive that we were accustomed to when visiting Ian at BDC, we were at the front door of River House in just about 9 minutes. "I'm nervous," I said to Ivan as we waited for someone to respond to the doorbell. Before Ivan had a chance to comment, a friendly face welcomed us. I didn't see Ian right away, but Martha, the house manager, told us that Ian was being changed and we could see him shortly. In the meantime, she introduced us to three staff and three residents who were sitting in the living room—a real living room with a large-screen television, a couch, a couple of recliners, pictures on the walls, and shades on the windows.

EARLY DAYS AT RIVER HOUSE

As soon as Ian saw us, he gave us the widest grin, followed shortly by his touching his nose, his sign to Ivan to recite the Willie Dreshen story. Ivan told him that he would tell the story later—he wasn't ready to embarrass himself in front of people we had just met. The staff gave us some privacy so we were able to spend time alone with

Ian. I don't know how much Ian understood when I explained to him that this was his new home, that we would be able to see him more often, that he would make new friends, and that he would get to ride in a van to his program every day. But he looked into my eyes and listened attentively.

Before we left we met his roommate, Alex, a short, but broad-shouldered and muscular young man. He seemed shy, but my thoughts still wandered to the possibility that he would hurt Ian. I explained to Martha that Ian often touched others, and expressed my concern that Alex might respond aggressively to Ian reaching out to him. "Don't worry about that," Martha said. "Alex may look like a football player but he's as gentle as a teddy bear."

As we were leaving, Barbara, another staff member, touched my shoulder as she reassured me: "I know you're worried about Ian, but we will take very good care of him." It's as if she had read my mind. Although I was excited about Ian living in this new house, years of witnessing the results of his being hurt at BDC clouded my joy. But I walked out the door more hopeful than I had been in decades that Ian had started a new and more joyful chapter in his life.

We visited again that weekend. So did Marsha, Steve, and Jay. Ian seemed to exhibit a calmer demeanor. We brought Elizabeth and Robert with us, who, by now, were used to being around people with odd mannerisms and a variety of physical and cognitive disabilities. I went out of my way to be friendly to everyone—the staff so they would take extra special care of my brother and to show my appreciation for what they do—and the residents so they wouldn't resent Ian and his visitors

The following Monday, Ian began attending the day program a short ride away from his home. "His home"—I loved that phrase. At the end of the day, Darryl, the team leader at the program, wrote the following letter to us and to staff:

Ian attended the RC-CLASS Program today. He was screened by the staff of the Program. He was somewhat

unsure of his new environment and reached out frequently to touch and grab things and individuals. But staff were on hand to help him with the transition. He shook hands with most of the staff present, spent the first part of his visit in the recreation and TV area where he joined some of the participants to watch an exercise videotape.

He was able to indicate to staff that he was hungry by constantly putting his hand in his mouth. Staff gave him lunch (sandwiches), and he ate three of them and a can of Ensure drink. We think that he can develop and maintain independent eating skills with the use of utensils such as a regular or built-up spoon. During lunch, he would not put on a paper bib, and as such had food stains all over his clothing. After lunch he went into the vocational skills area, where he worked with some of the participants to shred old newspapers for later distribution to the animal shelter. And by this time, he was more relaxed and less agitated.

He had a great visit and we look forward to working with him in some aspects of his ADL skills.

One day in the program and Ian already had a job. Ripping up newspapers—similar in some ways to his old hobby of tearing apart pieces of twine. Ian was already an expert in ripping stuff up, an activity that could keep him busy and happy for a long time. I laughed when I read that he refused to keep a paper bib on—one more thing to tear to shreds. Ian hated anything extra on his body— sleeves that reached to his wrists, mittens to keep his hands warm, bandages to cover an open wound, even shoes and socks. A bib tied around his neck would make him crazy.

Ian had lived at BDC from 1974 until 2000—more than a quarter of a century. At age 41, he was finally living again in a real home with a backyard, and he was cared for by kind people. Each day he would be driven to a center where he could participate in a program that provided physical, emotional, and cognitive therapy. That's

                    Harriet S. Mosatche

what I had always wanted for Ian. For the first time in a long time, I was optimistic that Ian would have a safe, healthy, and happy life.

MEETING IAN'S HOUSEMATES

After a short time, we got to know the five other people living in the house with Ian. Alex, Ian's roommate, really was a teddy bear as we had been told, and he loved playing catch and watching any kind of sports on television. His closet was filled with sports jerseys. Although he couldn't speak, he vigorously nodded his head up and down to indicate "yes" and from side to side for "no." He greeted us joyously, but without words. I didn't take it personally when he showed greater excitement when Ivan paid attention to him than when I did. He mainly interacted with Ian by observing him, at least when we were visiting.

Tom, the third male resident, had severe cerebral palsy and had lived at home with his parents and sister until his move to River House. He had his own room and a specially outfitted wheelchair since he had very limited muscle control. Although he couldn't speak, he understood everything that was said to him. He talked to his mother by phone every night, and he could answer her questions with various sounds that conveyed meaning to her. It took a few months before I realized that Tom had a great sense of humor—he laughed aloud when I made funny comments and particularly loved when I exaggerated or used sarcasm, such as when I noted that Ivan made the same comment about a new dining room table at least a dozen times.

The three women who lived at River House were Vicky, Susan, and Jessie. I never understood why Vicky was a resident in a group home. She was totally ambulatory, spoke well, and understood everything. She seemed more like a junior staff member than a resident. After a few months, Vicky moved to another group home, one that was more appropriate for her, but I was able to catch up with her at various Richmond functions, such as the Summer Carnival. She was replaced by Alice, who was also totally mobile but had obvious verbal and cognitive deficits. Instead of walking from place to place, she flitted around waving her arms. She craved attention and sidled up to everyone who visited. Like Ian, she sometimes hurt others because she wanted to be noticed, was not feeling well, or was frustrated.

Susan used a walker to get around and uttered a variety of phrases. I wasn't sure whether these phrases were ones that she memorized or had meaning for her. Some of the phrases included mild curses, which didn't bother me. If Ian could speak, I wouldn't care what words came out of his mouth. When Susan was sitting in the living room, invariably, she was paging though a magazine or catalogue. When I noticed that she had a very old copy of *O* magazine, I decided to subscribe to it so I could give it to her after I had finished reading it. The first time I handed her a new *O* magazine, she shrieked with glee. It was the best reaction I had ever gotten from a gift. Whatever Susan was looking at before I handed her the new *O* was tossed to the floor so she could immediately look through the new magazine. When I visited without a copy of the magazine, she turned away from me in disgust. Unfortunately, the magazine was only published once a month. I tried other magazines, but they were turned down—unless a picture of Oprah Winfrey was on the cover or somewhere in the magazine.

I had the hardest time getting to know Jessie. With multiple severe disabilities, she spent her time in her wheelchair and didn't react to a friendly hello or a compliment on the bows in her hair or the bright pink sweater she was wearing. She made noises, which her family probably understood but I could not figure out what she wanted or what would make her happier. She whined a lot, but every once in a while a smile would light up her face, which cheered everyone up. Although she was petite, she had a very strong grip— sometimes with her nails digging into your skin. When she held on to you, it was hard to get away. She didn't seem to know how to undo that grip, something I had experienced with Ian, too. Jessie had a couple of phobias that I learned about the hard way. Once

     Harriet S. Mosatche

when Ian spilled juice on the kitchen floor, I tore off a couple of sheets of paper towels to clean up the drops. At that moment, Jessie screamed—a high-pitched, piercing sound that stopped me cold. I didn't connect the tearing of the paper towels to the scream. While one of the staff comforted Jessie, another told me about several things that seemed to terrify her. Tearing of paper and turning on the microwave or dishwasher were the major catalysts of Jessie's fear. However, I learned that if you warned Jessie ahead of time—"Jessie, I am going to tear some paper towels now"—she remained calm. Unfortunately, from time to time, I forgot, and tore off a paper towel. The loud screeches reminded me quickly of my misdeed. The noises might have reminded her of some awful experience.

A GLORIOUS REUNION

About a month after Ian moved into River House, Ivan and I decided to arrange for Ian to visit Dad in his nursing home. More than a decade had passed since they had last seen each other. On the scheduled day, Ivan, Robert, Elizabeth, and I met Marsha and her family at Dad's nursing home. The weather was warm enough to take Dad out on to the terrace to wait for Ian's arrival. We didn't tell Dad what was about to happen—we wanted Ian's visit to be a surprise for him. Besides, even if we had told him, with his short-term memory basically absent, he would not have remembered. Marsha and I with our children waited in the lobby for Ian while our husbands entertained Dad—or more likely argued with each other about politics, an activity they both enjoyed. I told the aide who had brought Ian to the nursing home how much we appreciated what she had done. We wheeled Ian to the terrace, while telling him: "You're going to see Daddy. This is where he lives now."

Ian and Dad looked at each other— both wide-eyed with astonishment. Dad, who was typically very quiet and rarely initiated conversations any longer, said, with more enthusiasm than he had mustered in years, "Hi Ian!" Turning to the rest of us, he said: "Look who's here." As for Ian, he gave Dad the biggest smile and immediately reached out to him. He needed to be physically close to his father. Although so many years had passed and Dad's looks had changed, Ian had not forgotten. Tears of bittersweet joy welled up in my eyes. We had made the reunion happen—finally.

ADAPTING TO A NEW HOME AND NEW ROUTINES

Ian quickly adapted to life at River House. Each morning, he got dressed with assistance, ate breakfast, and rode in the white Richmond van to his day program. A mechanism at the back of the van allowed Ian in his wheelchair to be lifted into the vehicle. The chair was then strapped down. At least three of his housemates joined him on his trip to the program. Car rides had always been a special treat for Ian. He loved the sound and movement of the traffic and, if a car window was opened a bit, the wind created such a special effect for him that he vigorously rubbed his head and ears with excitement. Since Ian was attending a program outside where he lived, he had the opportunity to be a passenger in a moving vehicle every weekday.

When I toured the building where the Richmond day program was housed, I was pleased to see brightly colored walls, recliners, and a variety of toys, games, and supplies. On my first visit to see Ian while he was participating in his program, I observed Ian in a ball pool, just like the ones at kids' activity centers. Playing among the mass of light-weight colorful balls became Ian's favorite activity. Ian also learned to press buttons to activate appliances in the kitchen and continued to work at his job as a human paper shredder. He was a natural at that.

After a couple of months, Ian began to go on trips as part of his day program. I kept up to date on what he was doing through a composition notebook that went back and forth with him in his backpack. While staff at River House could use it to communicate something they needed the day program staff to know, almost all of the comments were written by Richmond staff at the day program. When I learned that Ian had gone to a museum, a swimming pool, a movie theater, or a shopping mall, I joked with him about it. The weekend after his visit to the Palisades mall (a place I still haven't visited although shopping is one of my hobbies), I said to him: "So you went on a shopping spree, I see. Did you get a new shirt?" I asked, using an exaggerated tone. "A new pair of pants? New shoes?" After each question, Ian would laugh while pointing to that item.

For each holiday, River House was gussied up with decorations. In December 2000, the house had a brightly lit Christmas tree in the living room along with a menorah in the window. Staff asked if it was okay for Ian to get Christmas presents. Of course, it was okay. I didn't want Ian to feel left out when everyone else was getting Christmas gifts. The staff were not allowed to receive gifts as a matter of policy to prevent them from showing favoritism toward particular residents whose families had given them something when others had not. However, I bought and wrapped gifts for the residents Alex, Tom, Jessie, Susan, and Alice, which I placed under the tree. I wrapped Ian's gift with bright paper, knowing that he would enjoy tearing it off. Each time we visited, I was glad to see the tree still standing upright with its lights and ornaments. I was concerned that Ian might try to pull something off the tree, knock it over, and start a fire. That's how my mind worked—and still does—because so many experiences with my family had trained me to prepare for the worst.

CONTINUING TO ADVOCATE FOR IAN

While I was really grateful to have Ian living in River House, Ivan and I continued to act as advocates on his behalf. No place was perfect, and if we could help to improve Ian's life, we were going to try to do it—gently, carefully, and usually tactfully. When I noticed a staff member sleeping on the job, I told myself: "This is very exhausting work. I need to let it go this time." I just made extra noise to encourage her to wake up. But after we discovered Louise asleep two more times, Ivan and I agreed that we had to bring it to the attention of her supervisor. In a private meeting, we mentioned what we had observed but also explained that we understand that sometimes the shifts are long and the work is tiring. Louise was not terminated for sleeping at work, but she was reprimanded. That was good enough for us. Fortunately, she would never be working alone with Ian. I hoped she would heed the warning and get her sleep in a more appropriate place.

We didn't want to make too many waves since Ian was relatively new to River House, just enough to make sure that Richmond administrators knew we would not look the other way when we saw something wrong. Ian was not easy to take care of—I recognized that sometimes he grabbed or pinched and that he didn't always cooperate. I made sure my advocacy was strategic and not constant. When I could ignore things, I did. Barbara, an aide at River House, had made a great first impression on me when I met her. She welcomed me warmly and seemed very kind. But after a short time, I started to notice that whenever Ian went near her, she immediately and harshly said to him: "Don't pinch" or "Don't grab me." It was like when you're told not to think about an elephant that you immediately think about an elephant. At one of the planning meetings for Ian, without naming anyone, I mentioned that instead of Ian reacting to that warning by not touching, he would be inspired to grab or pinch. A much better strategy, I suggested, would be for staff to praise Ian when he touched in a gentle way or to quickly maneuver out of Ian's reach but to do it subtly so that Ian would not see that as a rebuff. Some of the staff who worked with Ian, both at River House as well as in the program understood that, but some did not.

In one of Ian's first reports from his day program, Dennis described an effective way to get Ian to stop grabbing. He wrote:

Asking him firmly and at the same time making eye contact with him indicates to him that you would like for him to let go of you and produces a better result than trying to pull his arms off your person. He will release his grip at this point.

 Harriet S. Mosatche

That report also noted that Ian "continues to get very excited when staff members interact with him." How rewarding for me to read those words. I loved that he enjoyed spending time with me and the rest of our family, but our time with him was very limited so I wanted him to find joy being with people he saw much more frequently.

Since Ian was no longer able to walk and had spent most of his time in a wheelchair at BDC, it was good to see Ian confined to a wheelchair less and less of the time both at his day program and at River House. Instead, he sat in an armchair, a recliner, or a bean-bag chair as much as possible, which allowed for more freedom of movement. No professional was able to explain why Ian could no longer walk. We could speculate about possibilities, including brain trauma when he was beaten or muscle atrophy from disuse and lack of physical therapy after one or more of his beatings.

Although Ian was no longer ambulatory, he retained enough leg strength to push forcefully against the footplates of his wheelchair, breaking them repeatedly. His wheelchair spent a lot of time in the "Wheelchair Clinic," which meant that Ian had to use a loaner chair that was not adapted to his special physical needs. On occasion, when a loaner was not available and his wheelchair was not deemed safe enough to transport him, Ian had to stay back at River House while his housemates left for the day. In truth, they had become more than housemates—Alex, Tom, Alice, Susan, and Jessie were Ian's first real friends. At age forty-three, Ian finally had friends.

CHAPTER 22

The World Changes

The year 2001 was momentous—some events were very personal and meaningful, while others were shattering for many.

GOING PUBLIC

In June of 2001, my third book, *Girls: What's So Bad About Being Good? How to Have Fun, Survive the Preteen Years and Remain True to Yourself,* was published. Since Elizabeth and I had been working together as online advice columnists for the past few years, I asked her to contribute her ideas, and she wrote sections called "Liz Says." In many ways, this book was much more personal than anything else I had ever written. Recognizing that the written word could change attitudes, I decided to include a section titled, "No Family is Totally 'Normal' or Average or Typical." My advice in that section was not based on research I had done or statistics I had reviewed. It came from my need to reach out to tweens who were dealing with issues similar to what I had experienced at that stage of my life, at a time when I thought no one else had a family situation like mine. I wrote:

> Some kids find it easy to accept or talk about family members who are different. But most kids your age don't want anyone else to know about their family problems…If someone close to you is different, you feel embarrassed. To make

  Harriet S. Mosatche

*matters worse, lots of people out there, even in today's
sophisticated, informed world, make fun of people with
disabilities…If you've been hiding important family facts
from your friends, try sharing a little bit more with them.
Your true friends will accept you and your family, no matter
what they're like.*

I wish I had read advice like that when I was twelve. Elizabeth's
section on the topic was even more direct, personal, and insightful.
She wrote:

*My uncle Ian is mentally retarded and can't talk (he uses his
own form of sign language) or walk (he uses a wheelchair).
My family visits him two or three days a month at the group
home where he lives, and he's always happy to see us. While
I don't bring Ian up in conversations with friends, when a
related topic does come up, I will discuss his situation. I've
learned that I don't have to be embarrassed about Ian. He
is a part of our family…Sometimes he amazes me with
what he knows. Once, when my mother asked him what an
electroencephalogram was, he pointed to his head. It was
only then that I learned from my mom that the word means
a recording of electrical activity of the brain.*

UNIMAGINABLE HORROR

By the end of August, 2001, life was settling into a comfortable
routine. Then 9/11 happened. As I walked along Fifth Avenue
in Manhattan that beautiful sunny Tuesday morning, I noticed
that people were standing in the middle of the street looking and
pointing up ahead. I asked a man what was going on, and he said
that a plane had flown into the World Trade Center. That's when I
noticed smoke billowing from the building downtown. What a terrible accident, I thought, as I continued to walk to my office on 37th
Street. By the time I had taken the elevator to my floor and opened

the glass doors, a second plane had flown into the second tower. The chilling truth became immediately clear—it was no accident.

The building I worked in had large corner offices with almost floor-to-ceiling windows. Every horrifying thing was in clear view. I tried to call Ivan, first on my office phone and then on my cell, to let him know I was okay and to find out what he knew, but I couldn't get through. Meanwhile, I heard one of my co-workers screaming. Her husband worked on the 87th floor of one of the World Trade Center buildings. I took Elaine into my office with windows that faced north and east and did not have a view of the destruction unfolding. Ivan got through to me by phone and periodically called with updates about what was going on. He told me that he had assured our children that I was safe. I kept Elaine in my office throughout the day, preventing her from seeing the buildings collapse. Verna, one of my dearest friends and colleagues, helped me keep Elaine relatively calm. Unlike me, Verna is a deeply religious woman, and she used prayer that day in the most incredible way I had ever witnessed. Kneeling at Elaine's feet, Verna took hold of Elaine's hands and began to pray. Amidst the horror of the day, it was especially moving to watch an African-American Baptist pray with a white Jewish woman. Later that day, Elaine learned that her husband had walked down those many stairs to safety. Others were not as fortunate. The kind woman with twin teenage daughters who used to work as a cashier in the cafeteria of our office building had taken a better-paying job at Windows on the World. Her daughters lost their mother that day.

Hours went by. The subway system was shut down, bridges were closed. And my thoughts turned to Ian. How would staff get to River House? While Ian couldn't understand what had transpired and wouldn't worry about me in Manhattan, he would be affected by the sadness of those who took care of him. With so much suffering naturally occurring in the world, how could people knowingly inflict this kind of brutal pain and destruction on so many?

     Harriet S. Mosatche

Everything in the world felt different after 9/11. For a while, people were more helpful and friendlier, even to strangers. On my first plane trip a couple of weeks later, the captain asked the passengers to introduce themselves to each other. He didn't have to say a word about the terrorist attacks earlier that month—we understood that we could no longer be passive players when we traveled. That October, I was shocked to find out that one of my high school classmates was on the plane that went down in Pennsylvania. I did not tell Ian any of those stories or the many others from 9/11. For him, airplanes simply made a pleasurable sound and an interesting sight as they zoomed overhead. This time, his disability protected him from pain.

A PART OF THE COMMUNITY

While the annual reports I used to get from BDC were long—at least 30 pages—and filled with numerous goals described in excruciating detail (although never carried out), the Richmond "Integrated Plan Review" was half the length and contained few but clear and realistic goals. Ian's February 2002 plan included goals for Community (bagging shredded paper for distribution to an animal shelter with less need for verbal prompts), Communication (making choices), and Cooking (turning on an adaptive switch to activate a food processor). I figured that Ian would do well with the latter since turning on the switch would allow him to hear the buzzing sound of the machine. The report described the many trips that Ian went on during the year, including swimming at the local Y indoor pool, going to the animal shelter, shopping at grocery stores, visiting a game arcade, and eating out. Staff told us that he particularly loved the Chinese food buffet. After so many years of being hidden away inside an institution, Ian was regularly taking part in community outings. Only one kind of trip was off-limits to Ian, and I agreed with Dennis' assessment when he wrote:

Catch a movie with some of his peers—who would have thought that phrase would ever be used to describe one of Ian's activities?

When the weather was not too cold—since Ian still refused to keep his jacket sleeves down or gloves and a hat on—Ivan and I took him outside when we visited on the weekend. One narrow street leading away from River House was busy with two-way traffic so we couldn't walk on that street. Two of the streets adjacent to River House were short dead-ends with little to see. The fourth street meant navigating Ian in his wheelchair down a steep hill, no easy feat, but it was the best choice of our options. My husband didn't need to exercise on the days we visited Ian since preventing his wheelchair from tumbling forward down the hill and pushing the chair back up the hill required enormous stamina and strength, neither of which I had in the amount necessary. When we got down to the bottom of the hill, we could walk back and forth on a flat street with houses and often with people outside, which is what we did, over and over again. When we were ready to go back to River House, I would help Ivan by pushing him as he pushed the wheelchair up the hill. People stuck their heads out of their car windows to stare at the strange sight of a man in a wheelchair rubbing his head as another man pushed the chair up the hill followed by a laughing woman who had her hands pushing on the man's back.

We met some of the neighbors as we walked with Ian. Some made us feel welcome, while others just ignored us. One older woman told us to knock on her door if we needed a glass of water or anything else. She told us that she had a grandson who had to use a wheelchair, so I wasn't surprised at her empathy. We got to know one man particularly well since his house was at the bottom

     Harriet S. Mosatche

of the hill, and he was almost always outside, either fixing up his house or working on one of his cars. Ian noticed the many stages of the house's renovation and paid attention to our discussion of the addition of the deck and an additional floor. The house's owner, Mike, often stopped to say "hello" to Ian and to talk to us. When I thought back to how many people stared at Ian and called him names when I wheeled him in his stroller when he was four or five, I was relieved that we no longer had to face that, at least not in a direct way. Ian got particularly excited when Mike used water on a construction project or to clean one of his cars. Ian loved water, and if we walked close by, Ian could even get a few sprays of water. At the end of Mike's street, a highway was visible, so we typically spent a few minutes just watching through the fence as the cars whizzed by. If the day was somewhat windy, the joy for Ian was multiplied as the air whipped through his hair.

ADVOCATING ABOUT MEDICATION

In February of 2002, Ivan and I wrote a formal letter requesting that Ian's doctor reduce the dosage of Dilantin "with the goal of either eliminating its use, or perhaps changing to a different medication that has been developed since Ian was first put on Dilantin and that may have fewer side effects." We explained that Ian had not had a seizure in over 10 years and that, as far as we knew, no attempt had been made to reduce the dosage of Dilantin while Ian was at BDC. We ended our letter by stating: "We understand that there is a possibility that if the Dilantin dosage is reduced, Ian may start having seizures again." That sentence was important to reassure Richmond that we understood the risk of following through on our request, and that we were willing to take that risk on Ian's behalf. I had begun to be concerned about the long-term effect of Dilantin on Ian's health. Although it took a while, the Dilantin dosage was reduced and finally eliminated.

CHAPTER 23

Changing Communication

n 2002, Ian was 44 years old, although he looked much younger. I had taken on the role of mom to him, while Ivan had become like a father and Ian's strongest advocate. My children were adolescents—Elizabeth in her final year of middle school and Robert a high school junior—and continued to see Ian as their uncle although they acted more like his protective and loving siblings.

VISITING AND LEAVING

In July 2002, another book that Elizabeth and I co-authored was published. She had come up with the idea for the book, and we called it, *Getting to Know the Real You: 50 Fun Quizzes Just for Girls*. Even though she was busy with schoolwork and our book, most weekends she joined us when we visited Ian, while Robert, as a typical teenager, was often hanging out with a friend or sleeping in when we left for River House, so he was less likely to accompany us. But at least once or twice a month, he did join us. I made a point of not requiring that my children visit Ian since I did not want them to feel burdened. But they knew that I appreciated their making the time to visit when they did and how important Ian was to me. Without really meaning to, I'm sure I played the guilt card a bit, but I didn't feel bad about it since our visits took less than two hours out of their weekend. They often brought something to read or do—like homework or a travel game if they got bored. Learning to show compassion and give to others were important values in our family—these visits were opportunities to see those values in action as Ivan and I worked hard to entertain and care for Ian, and to take the time to pay attention to the other River House residents. Besides our stories and songs were funny, and, as long as Ian was feeling good and was enjoying the visit, our children did, too.

Although I felt more at ease about leaving Ian at River House than I ever had at BDC, I still often left wondering how Ian was faring in our absence. Would staff understand that he was thirsty? Would they know when he had a toothache? Would they try hard enough to make him smile? I did not share these feelings with my children. They could develop their own neuroses without my help.

AN OPPORTUNITY AND A GREAT LOSS

That summer, we learned about an opportunity for Ian to spend two weeks at a sleep-away camp for individuals with developmental disabilities. I talked to Marsha and Ivan about the pros and cons of residential camp for Ian. Ian would love to spend lots of time outdoors and maybe play in a lake. However, we were all concerned that he might be frightened by the new environment and strange people taking care of him. Would staff at camp fully recognize how he communicated his needs and understand that Ian didn't understand many of the dangers in the out-of-doors, particularly related to water? We decided that we didn't want Ian to go to camp that summer. We were assured he would have other opportunities in future years. While I was relieved that Ian wasn't going to camp that summer, I did wonder whether I was more concerned about Ian or about how uncomfortable I would be worrying for two weeks about all the dangerous things that could happen to him in the Catskills mountains.

Our family planned to spend the last two weeks that summer in Cape Cod, a vacation we had repeated for many years. We rented a condo and enjoyed the beach, tennis, pool, restaurants, and walking or biking trails. On Saturday night, at the end of our first week, the phone in our condo rang. Ivan picked it up. He didn't have to say anything. I knew the news wasn't good. Dad had just died. We packed up our stuff and drove home early the next morning. As was the case when Mom died, Marsha and I decided not to tell Ian. Dad would live on for Ian in the many stories Dad had told that were now part of our repertoire. The "Mrs. Miller" story was one of those that we all told, with each of us adapting the basic version to include parts that uniquely revealed our personal preferences. Mrs. Miller was a customer when Dad worked at a deli in Manhattan years before. Using an exaggerated German accent, Dad acted out Mrs. Miller giving her extensive order, ranging from two pounds of liverwurst to a pound and a half of braunschweiger to three-quarters of a pound of roast beef. Since Ian had roared with laughter as each part of the order was recited when I told the Mrs. Miller story, I lengthened it by adding side dishes (like potato salad) and my favorite desserts (such as pecan pie or a hot fudge sundae). Mrs. Miller, like Willie Dreshen, was a real and ordinary person in Dad's life, but both took on legendary status in our stories for Ian.

In the year that Dad died, the U.S. Supreme Court ruled in *Atkins v. Virginia* that executing people with mental retardation violates the Eight Amendment's ban on cruel and unusual punishment. The legal system was marching forward, slowly but surely, in protecting the rights of those with developmental disabilities.

NEW WAYS TO ENTERTAIN IAN

Early in his junior year of high school, Robert shocked us by telling us that he was going to perform a rap at a school performance. Our shy, white, Jewish teen was an aspiring rap star. He asked us to be his audience at home so he could practice before the performance. He used what I learned were "beats" from an existing rap and "sang" the lyrics he had written. They were witty, catchy, and a little scary. What impressed me most was the confidence with which he rapped—the swagger, the authentic hand gestures. Could Robert repeat that in front of his peers in the school cafeteria in a couple of weeks? It was one thing having your older, white parents watch

     Harriet S. Mosatche

you rap while sitting on your bed in your room and something entirely different performing in front of a large, diverse crowd of students. I asked if we could come to watch. "Parents aren't allowed," he quickly responded. Later, I learned that the mom of one of Robert's best friends had been in the audience. Audrey gave me a full report and said that Robert was the star of the evening wearing gold chains on his neck and wrist, the jeans hanging low, the white tank top tight over his fit 135 pound frame. After that first performance, Robert allowed us to come to a couple of other shows. I was prouder of him the first evening I watched him than I had been when I learned that he had become a National Merit Scholar finalist. He had taken a risk to learn to do something that did not come naturally, something way out of his comfort zone. And he was damn good!

Now that I knew that Robert could rap, I asked him to show Ian his new act. Robert asked if he needed to use a censored version. "Definitely not. Ian will love the curses." Besides, Ian wasn't about to repeat them. What a miracle it would be if he could. When Robert didn't get into his first choice college, Wharton Business School at the University of Pennsylvania, his guidance counselor found out that they had not looked kindly at the essay he had written about his transformation from smart but reserved student to popular rap star at school. Along with the application, Robert had enclosed the words and a CD with his original "College Application Rap." I had thought the essay and words to his original rap were unique and brilliant, but the Wharton Admissions committee evidently didn't agree.

PHONE CALLS

In June 2003, Robert graduated from high school, and on a hot, humid August day moved into his dorm at Duke University, which accepted him in spite of or maybe because of his rap. Before he left for school, he explained to Ian: "College is like the program you go to every day. You have different teachers and you learn lots of things. But my school is far away in North Carolina so I will not be coming home too often. I'll miss you, but I'll call you to talk to you."

While a phone call wasn't as good as an in-person visit, it would have to suffice while Robert was away at college. Since Ian touched his nose as a sign for Robert and Ivan as well as to indicate that he wanted to hear the Willie Dreshen story, we had to eliminate the latter two as possibilities before we were able to discern that Ian wanted to talk to Robert. When Robert did not answer our phone call, Ian seemed satisfied with just listening to Robert's voice mail message, so sometimes we called him five or six times during a single visit.

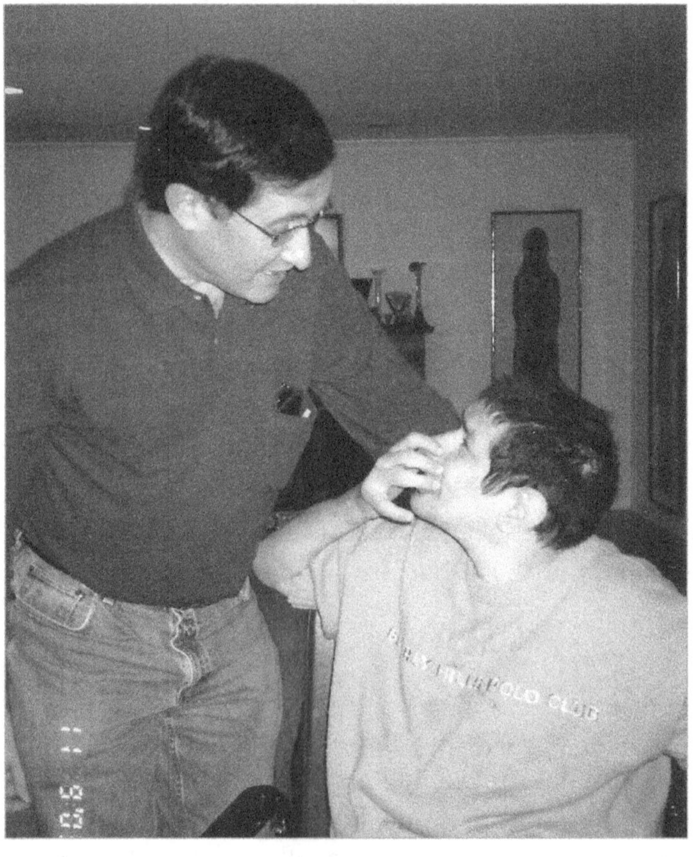

Ian communicating with Ivan

    Harriet S. Mosatche

Staff at River House called our house from time to time so Ian could hear us talk to him. We could hear him make noises indicating that he heard us, and staff told us that he was smiling. Sometimes, when I came home from work, the light was flashing on the answering machine. I smiled when I heard Ian "talking."

After Robert became a college student, Ivan was inspired to add a college chapter to the Willie Dreshen story. Now Willie took a psychology class taught by Dr. Mosatche. Ian pointed to me when he was asked who Dr. Mosatche was. Instead of a high school prom, Willie went to a college dance at which he met that beautiful girl who told him to blow his nose so she could understand what he was saying.

With Robert off at college, Elizabeth came up with new ways to entertain Ian. She had joined the high school's dance team and often demonstrated new steps for him. Because of her association with dance, Ian began to point to or touch his feet as a sign for Elizabeth. On occasion when she didn't join us in a visit to River House, Ian would point to his feet and we would need to explain where she was. Sometimes, we would call her on her cell phone, and she would talk to Ian for a minute or two. He didn't seem to understand the concept of holding the phone to his ear, so we put the phone on speaker until Ian lost interest in listening.

CHAPTER 24

A Social Man

an's quarterly and annual reports from the 2003-2004 period made it clear that he was a night owl. He was almost always the last resident at River House to fall asleep at night. Not surprisingly, he was the last one to wake up in the morning.

MAKING IAN LAUGH

Ian was acting like a college student—staying up late and sleeping in. On one of Robert's visits home, he asked Ian about that habit of late nights and sleeping in. "Did you have a party last night? You couldn't get up this morning? Drunk again?" Ian choked with laughter at those questions. I don't know whether Ian understood what "drunk" meant, but he definitely recognized that Robert was joking around.

When we found a new story or routine that Ian liked, we added that to our repertoire. "Are you going to college now? I heard you were drunk again last night" became lines that quickly elicited a grin or a laugh. When Ian was receptive to a story, I would improvise, making it more elaborate. "Are you hanging out with a fraternity? Spending any time in the library? Meeting any cute girls?"

Staff at River House looked for toys that Ian would enjoy and found one that had hanging chains that Ian could pull and which allowed him to feel the smooth chains against his skin. Although this toy didn't look very expensive, it cost about $70. I thought it was a great use for Ian's personal funds. Ian was very hard on his

 Harriet S. Mosatche

toys—when he grabbed at the metal chains, he was not gentle, and sometimes, he dropped the toy from his wheelchair. I requested that a half-dozen hanging chain toys be purchased. Since they had to be special-ordered, always having a couple in reserve meant that Ian would never be without the toy that meant so much to him. Toys go in and out of style, and I was concerned that the manufacturer might stop making them. If that ever happened, Ian would still have a stash of toys to tide him over until we figured out something that could serve as a replacement.

Ian's Program Plan Review covering a six-month period starting August 2003 indicated that Ian was receiving sensory stimulation therapy, arts and crafts therapy, music therapy, and aromatherapy on a weekly basis. And he was going on lots of trips, some of them an hour away, such as to the Brooklyn Museum of Art, the Brooklyn Botanical Garden, and Coney Island. How ironic that when Ian was living in Brooklyn for 25 years he was never able to explore the many diversions that the borough had to offer. Now that he was living in a different county, he began to visit some of Brooklyn's most interesting sites. I also learned that he went pumpkin picking. Knowing how much Ian loved sitting in the ball pool, I could only imagine the fun he had seeing and touching those bright orange pumpkins.

Ian's 2004 Annual Program Plan Review stated that Ian was "always thirsty" and drank "large amounts of fluids during the day." That was not the first time I had seen that written in his reports. Neither Ian's doctor nor I had considered the possibility that Ian's constant desire for water could be a symptom of an underlying health problem. Red flags didn't call out to me since Ian had always enjoyed playing with, being in, and drinking water. Besides, I wasn't looking for trouble.

STAFFING CHALLENGES

Staff turnover was high at River House as well as at the day program. Working with people with severe developmental disabilities is challenging and the salary certainly was not commensurate with the kind of physically demanding work staff were expected to do. I was impressed, however, with the many staff who were dedicated, hard-working, and kind. They compensated to a great degree for those who were less than stellar in their approach to their responsibilities and to the residents.

In June 2004, I received a letter from John introducing himself as the new residence manager for River House along with two other group homes. John noted that he had "extensive experience" in a variety of residential and day programs and looked forward to meeting family members. Although he made a great first impression on Ivan and me, our later impressions were much more negative. While he said the right things and promised that he was going to follow up on a variety of issues, he almost never seemed to get around to them.

Martha was the staff supervisor at River House and reported to John. Martha was often at River House when we visited, and she clearly cared about Ian and his housemates. But she did not seem to be able to deal in a firm manner with staff who weren't performing adequately. And she did not have the support of John (or even his presence). Martha was often busy with paperwork in the River House basement. I wanted her to spend more time upstairs so she could see what I saw—a staff member asleep or expressing anger loudly, residents sitting bored while the television played a program that interested staff but not residents. Ian's roommate Alex loved everything related to sports, and Tom enjoyed game shows such as *Jeopardy* and *Wheel of Fortune*. But invariably, a Lifetime drama was on with staff watching intently. Ivan was the one who usually asked politely if he could change the channel, maybe to a NCAA game during March Madness, which he knew Alex would love.

Although we did our share of advocating for Ian and the other residents—sometimes viewed as complaining—we also tried to serve as role models—reading books aloud, singing songs, telling jokes, and playing catch with light foam balls. I never forgot

     Harriet S. Mosatche

how tough it is to stay engaged and to handle all the mundane and difficult tasks that are part of working with individuals with severe disabilities. However, I also knew that everyone, not just the residents, are more likely to become moody, aggressive, or even self-abusive when they are bored. Alice, Susan, and Alex were at least partly ambulatory, so they could leave a room or walk over to a staff member for attention. But Ian, Tom, and Jessie were unable to move their wheelchairs independently, so they were the ones who most needed the stimulation to come to them and in a form that was positive, not the sound of loud talking or screaming on television. Sometimes when I visited, Ian was wearing a t-shirt that was wet and full of holes since, when he was bored, he chewed on his shirt. He also took off his shoes and socks and picked at the scabs on his feet. That's what people do when they're bored—they have to find something to stimulate them. Ian didn't chew his shirt when we were telling him about Willie Dreshen's operations or Mrs. Miller's deli order. He didn't pick at his skin when he listened to Elvis Presley or James Brown, his favorite singers. I never forgot how much better Ian was being cared for at his group home than he had been at BDC. But I never stopped wanting his life to be even better and was always alert to conditions that could make his situation worse.

Although we had hardships in our family, many good things did happen, and they were cause for big celebrations. In July 2004, my niece Sherry married Jeff, a friendly, kind young man whom she had met at college. Jeff passed the "Ian test." Jeff seemed comfortable greeting Ian, even shaking his hand when they first met. That might seem like a very ordinary thing, but treating Ian with respect and without fear was not typical and a very big deal to me and to my sister.

CHALLENGE OF THE MOVE PROGRAM

In the fall of 2004, Ian joined the *Move* program at Richmond. Ivan and I had strongly advocated for Ian's participation in this program since it was designed to increase mobility. Transitions to new environments were always difficult for Ian, and this particular change, for some unknown reason, was very stressful for him. He began to pull people's hair and pinch fellow group members and staff, behaviors that had decreased markedly since he had arrived at River House. The Move program did not have staff to deal with Ian's aggression so he returned to the day program he had been in before. Immediately, he became his old calm, friendly self. I was disappointed that Ian's involvement was short-lived since I had heard so many positive reports about the Move program and had already envisioned Ian standing up and taking steps. Maybe Ian would get another opportunity to join the program at a later date.

In spite of this one "failure," Ian's Annual Program Plan Review stated that, "Ian is a very social man who enjoys interactions with staff and his peers." Ian's warmth and smile had always had the power to melt my heart, and now others, too, were able to perceive those special qualities in him. That was deeply gratifying.

Harriet S. Mosatche

CHAPTER 25

Old Memories and New Activities

While I was generally satisfied with Ian's experience in his day program, I was not happy that he was receiving various forms of therapy only sporadically. When a contract ended with a vendor supplying physical and occupational therapy, it took months for Richmond to contract with another agency and for Ian to receive much-needed therapy that would prevent further atrophy of his muscles. Back to our role as advocates—Ivan made phone calls and I talked at meetings, requesting these services.

DR SEUSS MAKES A REAPPEARANCE

At one of the meetings I attended to review Ian's goals and discuss the use of his personal funds, I suggested the purchase of Dr. Seuss books. Although I had not read those books to Ian in years, it was worth seeing whether they still held the same sway over him that they had when Marsha and I read to him every night at home. Also, others could read to him when we weren't there—that was definitely a plus. Although Dr. Seuss books are considered children's literature, Ivan and I had always personally enjoyed reading those books to Robert and Elizabeth when they were younger. Maybe Ian's housemates would also like hearing the rhymes and nonsense that uniquely came from the imaginative mind of Dr. Seuss.

When I first read one of those books aloud to Ian at River House, he remembered many of the words even though he had not heard those stories since he had left home decades earlier. When I paused so that Ian could complete a phrase with gestures, he did so with remarkable accuracy, touching his chest before he heard the word "heart" or rubbing his head for "hat" or pointing to his eye for "see." *Horton Hatches the Egg* had been and remained a favorite, and when I read the line, "… And the icicles hung, From his trunk and his…", Ian bent down to grab his feet. Ivan not only entertained Ian with his dramatic rendition of *Fox in Sox*, but Ian's housemates Alex and Tom, too, loved hearing the story. Ivan's and Ian's favorite part was: "… when tweetle beetles battle with paddles in a puddle, they call it a tweetle beetle puddle paddle battle …"

By this time, Ian had been living at River House for several years, and we were no longer embarrassed about acting in foolish ways. Our goal was to make Ian and the other residents laugh, and they did. Ian never tired of Dr. Seuss and could listen for long periods of time, one book after another, with Elizabeth, Ivan, and I taking turns reading. Sometimes, I needed to remind Elizabeth to speak in a louder, more dramatic way, since Ian reacted best to that kind of recitation. When she was too soft-spoken, Ian made it clear with gestures and grunts that she had to turn up her performance a notch or he would take the book from her to give to me.

INCLUDING PHYSICAL EXERCISE IN OUR VISITS

We tried to make physical exercise part of each of our visits. Since Ian reacted well to rhythmic movements and sounds, I created a basic exercise routine that he became comfortable with and we could do together. "Reach for the ceiling, one, two, three, four. Touch the floor, one two, three four," and then I could add anything else I could think of to get Ian to move. I also taught Ian to do a dance, one he could do sitting on his bed or in a chair, one adapted from a childhood favorite song. It went like this:

     Harriet S. Mosatche

Brother, come and dance with me.
Both my hands I offer thee.
Right foot first, left foot then.
Round and round and back again.
With my hands, go clap, clap, clap.
With my feet go tap, tap, tap.
Round and round and back again.

Ian liked the melody and seemed proud that he could fill in the words by reaching to take my hands, clapping his hands, and tapping his feet at the appropriate times. And it was an opportunity for him to move. He didn't always point with the correct leg in response to "right foot first, left foot then," but when I said, "Other leg," he quickly corrected himself.

One of the opportunities that Ian had for listening to music and dancing was at a festival organized each June on the grounds of the main building at Richmond. Tables were set up for each group home and for the residents of other facilities. Bands, a roving clown, animals such as rabbits and ponies, balloons, face-painting, and a barbecue created a party atmosphere for residents, staff, and family members. Ivan and I made sure that Ian participated in as many of the activities as possible, from getting all of his favorite foods to visiting with the clown to sitting close to the stage when the rock and roll band was playing Elvis songs. Each year, one resident from another group home sought me out to dance with him. I didn't dance too long with Ben because Ian got jealous that I was giving my attention to someone else. The only person Ian didn't mind my dancing with was Ivan. In fact, Ian grinned as he pushed Ivan and me together so we could dance, making a spectacle of ourselves in public.

CHAPTER 26

Five Years and Counting

By 2005, Ian had been living at River House for five years and memories of BDC were becoming more distant. We continued to visit Ian every weekend, except when a vacation, a business trip, or illness made that impossible.

That year, a new President and CEO came to Richmond. I was hopeful that he would deal with some of the issues that needed to be addressed. Staff turnover and the frequent use of per diem staff was a problem, and in an October 2005 letter to "Members of the Richmond Family," he noted that he recognized that issue, particularly with regard to nurses. He also stated that Richmond had purchased a digital camcorder, which he hoped could be used "to create DVDs of families introducing their loved ones to our staff members." A wonderful idea, but as far as I knew, that never happened.

SENSORY STIMULATION

When we visited Ian at River House, he wanted us all to himself. Sometimes staff would come in to his room to put away clothing or ask us a question. Ian made it very clear this was his time with his family. He would grunt or even push them a bit to make his point firmly. Ian wanted to get back to the routines, the songs, the praise, the stories, the laughter, the silliness that made up our private time with him.

When Ivan wasn't telling Ian a story or talking to staff, Ivan often fell asleep on the floor of Ian's bedroom. His position seemed incredibly uncomfortable to me, his head leaning against the side of Alex's bed and his legs stretched out in front of him. Within a couple of minutes of Ivan scooting down to the floor, he would be snoring. Sometimes, Ian didn't mind being ignored by Ivan, but at other times Ian would gesture to me to wake Ivan up or he would grunt in Ivan's direction, indicating very clearly that sleeping during a visit was not acceptable. Even if Ian had wanted stimulation, the noise of Ivan's snoring was not what Ian had in mind. Years later, Ivan found out that his propensity to fall asleep amidst noise and light was due to his severe sleep apnea.

One of Ian's goals for 2005 was to experience enhanced tactile stimulation. An activity introduced to Ian as part of his goals was choosing oils and lotions for massaging his hands. I liked to imagine Ian giggling as he rubbed the lotions not only on his hands but probably through his hair as well when he rubbed his ears and head with glee.

Ian's 2006 Individualized Service Plan report indicated that he loved the movie, "Catwoman" and would watch it over and over. Car-racing television programs were also on his preferred list. Action and that roaring noise—a perfect combination for Ian.

ELIZABETH'S PROJECT

In Elizabeth's senior year of high school, she had her first boyfriend, and he was kind enough to come to River House with us a few times to meet Ian and to play his guitar and sing for him. Peter was the first friend whom she trusted to meet her special uncle. Having Peter entertain at River House was kind of a pilot phase for Elizabeth's Girl Scout Gold Award project. She had been a Girl Scout since the age of five, and the Gold Award would be the culmination of that experience. Elizabeth's project was based on a need she had identified from her observations at River House. She had noted that when she visited Ian, the residents were usually in the living room watching television, not a very stimulating experience.

After explaining her idea to and getting approval from the Director of Volunteers at Richmond, she organized a live entertainment program for Sullivan House, the group home that Ivan and I had visited five years earlier when we were trying to find a new place for Ian to live. Sullivan House was conveniently located for the friends who would be joining her in implementing the project. She asked Peter and several of her friends to join her whenever they were available to provide entertainment at Sullivan House. She asked me to assist her in training these volunteer high school students so they would go into the group home prepared for their experience—that they would understand that residents might grab them, that they might drool, that they might say inappropriate things, or even that they might just ignore their presence. As part of the training, Elizabeth helped her peers understand that even those who couldn't talk or join in the singing were still capable of enjoying the music and seeing new visitors.

I joined Elizabeth and her friends on one of their visits to Sullivan House, but not right away—this was her program, not mine.

     Harriet S. Mosatche

I watched Peter play a couple of Elvis Presley songs, Gary juggle, Maddie and Eryn sing, and Elizabeth dance. I couldn't have been prouder of her leadership and compassion. Because Elizabeth wanted the program to continue and perhaps even expand to other group homes, she created a how-to booklet, which she gave to her school guidance counselor as well as to the Director of Volunteers at Richmond. I don't know whether anyone else ever used the model she had created, but I hoped others would replicate the program. Creating music and fun for the residents of group homes was so much better than having them sit passively while the television blared. As a result of the project, Elizabeth earned the highest award in Girl Scouting, a Gold Award.

VISITS TO OUR HOUSE

Since Robert came home from college infrequently, Ian grew very excited each time he showed up. Summer was great for Ian since Robert had taken a local job teaching tennis and was able to visit River House often. However in August 2006, both Robert and Elizabeth left for college. It was the first time since Ian had moved to River House that he would not see Elizabeth weekly. She had explained that she was going to college—"like Willie Dreshen," she noted, referring to Ian's favorite story. But she would be back in a few months. I knew that would seem like forever to Ian, but Ivan and I (and Marsha, Steve, and Jay) would try our best to make Ian happy in the absence of our children.

During this time, Ian came to our house about once a month for a visit. On one of those occasions, when Ivan had left bottles of vitamins and minerals on the kitchen table, Ian began to pick them up. I was cutting up Ian's sandwich, and Marsha began to read the labels—Calcium, Vitamin C, and Mature Multivitamins—with a loud comical voice. Ian started to laugh. A new routine was born. Whenever he came to our house in the future, I brought out the containers, and asked Ian about Ivan's Mature Multis, a surefire way to elicit laughter.

When the weather was decent during Ian's visits to our house, we rolled him in his wheelchair up and down our street, an easy flat one with little traffic. When my friend Judy who lives on our street was home, she came out to walk with us for a few minutes, always complimenting Ian on something he was wearing or on his hair style. He loved the attention. I told Ian that she worked with children who were blind. That fact became a new question in my test for Ian. "What does Judy do?" I would ask, and Ian would immediately point to his eyes. Whenever we walked Ian up and down our street, he would point to Judy's house, making sure I knew that he wanted to visit with her.

We rarely used our outdoor furniture, but before Ian visited if the weather was perfect for an outdoor meal, we cleaned the table and chairs and gave Ian his lunch outside. Outdoors, Ian could be as messy as he desired. There were plenty of animals in the backyard that would eat up whatever dropped to the ground. After lunch, Ivan or I would push Ian in his wheelchair close to the woods, saying: "We're going into the forest now." Ian found that hysterical, and as hard as it was to maneuver the chair over the uneven lawn, we weren't going to miss an opportunity to make Ian laugh. Sometimes, Marsha and Steve or Jay would join us at our house, so we all took turns pushing the wheelchair around.

In the fall of 2006, I noticed a change—Ian seemed sad on many of our visits. When we picked up Jay to join us, he also saw the change in Ian's demeanor. No matter what we tried, and we used every trick in our repertoire, Ian just seemed down to us. Was he feeling sick? Was he afraid of someone or something? We got our answer when Elizabeth visited Ian at Thanksgiving. Suddenly, his mood lightened. He had missed her terribly. He had gotten used to those weekly visits, and perhaps he had thought that she had disappeared from his life the way his mother and father had. After that visit, Ian was back to his old cheerful self. Elizabeth could now be gone for months at a time, but he was reassured that she would be back. Ian did have a sense of time. On those rare occasions

     Harriet S. Mosatche

when Ivan and I missed a weekend, Ian would greet us with even greater enthusiasm than usual—smiling broadly and holding us close. "Didn't you know we'd be back?" I would ask.

CALLS FROM IAN

One of the goals or "valued outcomes" described in Ian's 2006 report was:

> *"Ian would like to dial the phone number and communicate on the telephone with his family on a weekly basis."*

I liked the way the goal described Ian's preferences, not just some bureaucratic goal someone had set for him. By providing hand-over-hand assistance, Ian was able to push the correct buttons on the River House telephone to reach us.

> *Staff will wait to see if one of Ian's family members answers the phone and staff will give Ian the phone when his family has agreed to speak with him. Staff will assist by either holding the phone for him next to his ear or by using the speakerphone function. Staff will ask Ian if he is done using the phone when they think the conversation is over. If he responds that he is done, staff will take the phone away and speak with the family member to confirm that the conversation is through.*

Although Ian was in a much better place in 2006 than he had been a decade ago, I had become increasingly concerned about the lack of stimulation at River House as well as the hostile way some staff acted toward us and the perfunctory manner in which they cared for the residents. I was outraged when I came into Ian's home and found him soaking wet, having not been changed for many hours. Or when Tom's head was stuck in an uncomfortable position in his wheelchair because he couldn't move his head on his own due to his cerebral palsy. Or when Jessica was sitting next to the television instead of in front of it, which meant she couldn't watch it. Ivan and I were continually trying to find the right balance between complaining and letting things go.

I wasn't totally surprised when Ivan answered the phone one evening and heard from a man who wouldn't give his name but described details of physical and emotional abuse toward Ian and others, particularly Jessica, at River House. While he wouldn't give the name of the staff member, he said that when a particular staff member was angry, she had thrown a shoe at Ian's head, and that the staff supervisor knew about these incidents. We did not know how this man had gotten our phone number, but it didn't really matter. What was important were the allegations, which Ivan immediately reported to a top Richmond administrator who assured us that they would be looked into. The result was that they could not find support for the allegations, but the outcome for Ivan and me was that we would be watching much more carefully. I suspected that there was more than a grain of truth to those allegations.

CHAPTER 27

A Variety of Changes—
Good, Bad, and Ugly

The year 2007 marked important changes in our family. After four years at Duke, Robert graduated, but not yet sure of the direction he wanted his life to take, he decided to spend time traveling. Before he and four friends from high school began their journey through South America, Robert explained to Ian that he would not be able to see or call him for a while but that he would be returning with lots of interesting stories.

CHANGING ENVIRONMENTS

At age 48, Ian started attending a day program in Mount Kisco, the most attractive setting he had ever been in and one that would give him more opportunities for stimulation and learning. His annual report indicated that he had adapted well to the transition where the focus was on "life enhancement through skill development." Who could argue with that mission?

My big change occurred in July of 2007 when I left the Girl Scouts organization where I had worked for more than 17 years. I started a consulting company, which allowed me the flexibility, control, and creativity that I desired. I would now be able to attend meetings related to Ian's care and have time to visit him during the week if we had weekend plans. Since Ivan was self-employed, it was a bit of a financial risk for us, but it was a change I needed to make for my health and sanity.

That year, Ian visited a Barnes and Noble bookstore (I hoped they showed him all the Dr. Seuss books there), Kensico Dam, an amusement center in our town, several local public libraries and malls, a YMCA swimming pool, and the Chinese buffet (which continued to be a favorite). A report about Ian described him as "very friendly" and stated that he could:

> *"… initiate interaction by maintaining eye contact or holding onto the person…He continues to murmur as a technique of engaging/responding while occupied in conversation, frequently demonstrating understanding of the concepts of the dialogue."*

Ian was finally recognized for what he could do, not just for his deficits. Of course, there were some behavioral issues, as noted in that same report:

> *Ian continues to abruptly remove various clothing items; however the frequency of this behavior has decreased. He will sometimes exhibit behaviors such as pinching his peers and attempting to squeeze their arms. When this happens, staff need to redirect his attention to another object or activity…He does not like wearing socks or shoes and will remove them whenever possible.*

For that year, Ian had four "Valued Outcomes, one of which focused on going shopping in the community.

> *Ian would like to go to the store to make community pur-chases…Staff will transport Ian out in the community to a store that he wants to go to (they will give him a choice of two stores, …and he will grunt or smile when staff names a store he wants to go to). They will take Ian to a store and give him a choice of two items…(he will grunt or smile at*

 Harriet S. Mosatche

the item that he wants to buy). Staff will take Ian over to the checkout counter. They will use the hand-over-hand method to help Ian pay for the item he chooses to buy. Staff will transport Ian back to the house after he is finished with his community outing.

The other goals also relied on Ian's grunts and smiles to indicate his preferences. In that way, Ian was able to choose a snack to eat or a toy to play with, or to tell staff when he was tired of working with thera-bands, which were used to strengthen Ian's upper body. One of Ian's new goals was in the area of personal hygiene, namely, "Ian would like to file his nails, with staff assistance." I don't know how much Ian really wanted to file his nails, but he probably enjoyed the finger bath that began his manicuring session.

ADVOCACY AND INVESTIGATION

Ivan and I continued to advocate for Ian to receive the services both in his day program and at River House that had been authorized for him. After repeated inquiries, we were told that the outside agency that had been contracted to provide occupational and speech therapy did not have enough professionals so Ian could not receive those services. Since the agency had not fulfilled their contract, why wasn't another agency hired? I tried to be patient, but as time went by, Ian's skills weakened. His muscles had already atrophied due to the lack of exercise and therapy over past decades. He couldn't afford to waste more time waiting for needed treatment. That was not the only issue for Ian and the other residents. I was growing increasingly concerned about the lack of stimulation at River House on the weekend, and about how some staff treated the residents, including ignoring their distress, acting annoyed when they had to clean up a mess, and not changing the residents frequently enough. If they acted that way when family members were around, what were they doing when we weren't there? Some staff were caring and hard-working, but I worried about the ones who weren't.

Ivan and I got to know the families of the other residents, and in particular, Tom's mom, dad, and sister, who visited as frequently as we did. We assured them if we noticed anything amiss with Tom, we would be sure to let them know, and they agreed to do the same with regard to Ian. In September 2007, I learned that a new investigation was begun after an anonymous letter had been sent to the Richmond CEO indicating that abuse was occurring at River House, including hitting, food being thrown out when residents did not finish eating quickly enough, and showering not done consistently. The letter writer made it clear that the abuse had gone on for some time.

As I read through the 13-page Investigative Report that Richmond had commissioned, tears filled my eyes. I had had such high hopes for Ian's life in a group home, and now this litany of abuse was revealed. The report I received included Ian's name, but to maintain the necessary confidentiality, the staff and other residents were described with numbers. These are some of the disturbing facts related to Ian that were included in the report:

- Direct Service Provider (DSP) 7 "admitted hitting Ian" and stated that DSP 2 would "plop (roughly push) Ian in a chair, she speaks mean, has seen her hit Ian when he squeezes Individual 3's arm."
- DSP 4 "indicated in conversation and in writing that she has witnessed DSP 2 refuse to finish feeding Ian because he makes noises, has hit Ian when he makes noise, screams at him and will slap him in the face (hard), and slap his hands hard when he tries to get his belt off…She has witnessed DSP 1 slapping Ian when he is pulling at his belt… (and) slapping Ian's hands when (he tried) to reach for staff and other residents." She noted that when Ian was "smacked in the face…it sounded hard but did not leave a red mark."

     Harriet S. Mosatche

- "DSP 3 witnessed DSP 2 being rough. She will push Ian hard in his chair when transferring him, shout at him, poke his head or hit his hands and feet with an open palm when he 'growls,' slap his hands when he is trying to get in his belt, and shove medication down his throat…" She would also slap Ian on the head "as she walks by."
- DSP 5 stated that she "witnessed DSP 6 being rough…she (would) push his (Ian's) arm and talk out loud…Then Ian (would) be upset and make noise." DSP also noted that DSP 6 "will sometimes push him (Ian) roughly in his chair and with open hand will slap him if his grunting annoys her."
- DSP 6 "stated that staff should bring up allegations against the clients. Ian is spiteful and stubborn."
- DSP 8 witnessed DSP 1 "give Ian a hard slap on the back and then asked him to give her a hug, which he did."
- "DSP 9 witnessed DSP 2 talk loud and firm when Ian made a sign for drink, DSP 2 said loud and firm, 'No way, no drink now.'" DSP 9 "stated that she has heard DSP 5, 2, 3, and 1 yelling at Ian."
- "DSP 10 has witnessed DSP 2 speak roughly with Ian."

Although it appeared that Ian and Jessica received most of the physical abuse, the other housemates did not escape unscathed. One resident was repeatedly called "Big Head" by staff, told "to mind his business" when he interrupted them, and yelled at when he would grind his teeth. At times, he was left in his room for hours. Staff hit another resident on her hand, including at least one time outside the house, and pulled her hair when she wouldn't get up readily for her shower. When another resident "was hit under the chin" by a staff member, another one said in an interview: "…she was hit hard but not enough to knock out teeth." That same resident was also treated in a "hard manner," including shaking her up and down and swaying her from side to side.

MORE CHANGES, BUT NOT ENOUGH

While I was relieved that this terrible situation had been uncovered, I felt guilty that I hadn't realized the scale of the abuse and done more to stop it sooner since I had certainly seen signs of neglect and emotional maltreatment. But more than that I was angry. Angry that the house supervisor and residence manager, out of loyalty to their staff or neglect of their responsibilities, either didn't know what was going on under their noses or chose to do nothing with what they had observed or were told. Angry with staff who had witnessed abuse but remained silent. Angry that people who were charged with caring for people with severe disabilities had been so physically and emotionally abusive over such a lengthy period. Angry that the previous investigation hadn't been thorough enough to uncover the truth and stopped the pervasive abuse at River House earlier.

Ivan and I swore that we would be more vigilant in the future—seeing something amiss would be followed by action. We, along with family members of other residents, requested and participated in a meeting with the top administrators. They had taken some immediate action, such as firing DSP 2 and the house supervisor, who had been at River House since it was established in 2000. While I had always liked her, and she had personally been great with Ian, I couldn't argue with Richmond's decision to let her go since she had not taken action when she observed and heard about abuse. But we wanted further assurance that Richmond would implement better procedures, particularly real oversight, so that we would not be revisiting the same kind of situation in the future. Was there no end to what Ian had to endure?

At the end of October, the assistant vice-president of Clinical Services and Support at Richmond wrote a letter to the families of the River House residents. She described some of the steps that would be taken, including better supervision and training, family meetings with and without staff, and the implementation of inter-esting recreational activities at home and in the community. What

     Harriet S. Mosatche

I most appreciated was the honest and open apology. The letter ended with: "…I extend my humblest apologies to Tom, Jessica, Ian, Alice, Susan, and Alex; and to each of you. I will make every effort to make and keep things right."

A new staff supervisor was hired for River House in January 2008, but she didn't last long, not even long enough to leave any kind of impression on me. John, the Residence Manager who, in my opinion, had overstayed his welcome, either left of his own accord or was fired. One of the criticisms of him that staff had made during the 2007 abuse investigation was that if he been present more of the time, things might not have reached a crisis point. He claimed that he knew nothing of the abuse. That may well have been true since John was rarely present, regardless of when I came to visit, but that was no excuse.

That June, Richmond finally cut ties with the agency that had failed to adequately provide speech, occupational, and physical therapy to residents, and contracted with another agency. A new Residence Manager also began working at River House that month. She came with two decades of experience working with people with developmental disabilities. Ivan and I both took advantage of the invitation to interview her, and we were duly impressed, as were the families of other residents who met with her. She was friendly with everyone and listened attentively to what we told her about our loved ones who were under her care. Many promises had been made in the past by one person after another, so I remained skeptical about how effective she would be but I was open. Kathleen did seem to try, but running the house was more than she could handle. Before a year had gone by, she, too, had left River House.

CHAPTER 28

Riding the Roller Coaster with Ian

n July, Robert returned from his 10-month trip throughout South America. But before he came back to the United States, Ivan, Elizabeth, and I visited him in Ecuador. Robert had just finished spending a month in the jungle, a community service project of sorts, in which he lived with a family and a monkey. When Robert told us about the monkey sharing his fleece jacket nightly as their pillow, I realized that I had to remember the details so I could tell them to Ian when we got back home.

STORIES FROM SOUTH AMERICA

While in Ecuador visiting Rob, we took a cruise to the Galapagos Islands where, inadvertently, I had an experience that became one of Ian's favorite stories of all time. We were guided along a rocky path where native birds, with the wonderfully silly name of blue-footed boobies, hatched their eggs. Although I tried to avoid stepping anywhere near the nests, evidently, my left foot got just a bit too close, and the mother bird swooped down to give me a sharp nip on my ankle. Since I had received by an amazing coincidence a fake stuffed blue-footed booby from a work colleague some time before that, I had a prop for telling my story to Ian. I gave Ian a dramatic rendition, complete with my high-pitched screech when the bird found its target. Ian roared with laughter, almost losing his breath.

The story never lost its power. All I had to ask Ian was: "What did the blue-footed booby do to me?" and he would react with a broad grin and then reach down to touch my ankle.

Through his many months living in South American, Robert had become fairly fluent in Spanish. Since Ian liked accents and foreign languages, I asked Robert to tell Ian the Willie Dreshen story in Spanish on one of his first visits to River House after arriving back in the United States. Although Ian did not understand Spanish (as far as I knew), he was able to fill in the missing words to the story with gestures and sounds. Robert could never leave the story alone and entertained all of us with additions and changed endings. In one of the Spanish versions of the story, the girl at the dance came home with Willie Dreshen "only because of my flawless Spanish; she couldn't tell I was a gringo in the dark dance hall." We all laughed when Robert translated for us.

SHOWING WHAT HE KNOWS

Although Ian couldn't use spoken language, he constantly showed us what he knew and how his mind worked. When Elizabeth took a developmental psychology class in college, I demonstrated to her that Ian understood the concept of "object permanence." With Ian focused on me, I hid a ball under his blanket while he was watching. Young babies act as if the object has disappeared when it is no longer in sight. On the other hand, Ian recognized that the ball continued to exist and immediately searched under the blanket to recover the object. Ian was not fooled, even by more elaborate demonstrations, such as a ball rolling under the bed or a ball first being placed under a blanket and then under a pillow. Ian could always find the absent object under the last hiding place.

The longer Ian lived at River House and attended Richmond's day program, the more staff recognized how much he knew. His June 2008 Individualized Service Plan report stated that: "Ian is very affectionate and caring. He is very sociable and reaches out to interact with people. He is very alert and aware of his environment. He loves one-on-one attention." Even though River House proved to be problematic in other ways, it was heartening that staff recognized Ian's strengths.

Ever since Ian had started to live at River House, his social world kept growing larger. Robert's high school friend Annie stayed with us for the month of October, after leaving her job in Massachusetts and before starting a trip to China, an opportunity to feel closer to her Taiwanese-born mother who had died when Annie was 16. As we got to know her better, she became not just a friend, but a part of our family. Annie spent a lot of time with us, including celebrating Thanksgiving with our family each year and other holidays as well. Annie interacted easily with Ian when he visited at our house. Although I tried not to judge people who felt uncomfortable with or avoided Ian, those who showed compassion and respect scored a whole lot of points with me. Annie once told me that one of her fondest Christmas memories was from when she visited River House in 2008. She told me:

> *We arrived to have dinner with everyone and celebrate the holidays with Ian. Honestly, I was nervous and scared. At first, I stood in the corner or sat on the sofa without really speaking to anyone. I had worked in a clinic for a year, assisted with code blues, but I was nervous about speaking to Ian and his housemates. I remember when you started dancing and singing with them. People were laughing, cheering, and dancing themselves. Ian was moving in his chair, and I realized that it's okay for me to act silly and have fun because to be part of pure happiness is such a beautiful thing. That night Ian showed me humility and that I don't need to be serious all the time.*

One of Ian's new Valued Outcomes for 2008 was to wash and dry his hands independently. His report indicated that "Ian just recently began working on this outcome but has done well to this point. He

    Harriet S. Mosatche

enjoys playing in the water and is able to dry his hands most of the time with staff assistance." As had been the case for years, Ian's report also indicated that Ian "enjoys drinking large quantities" of water. Maybe I should have questioned whether that indicated a possible health issue, but I didn't.

Jay continued to visit at least once a week and we did the same, usually at different times so Ian could enjoy more family time. Marsha and her husband Steve visited less often, and occasionally their son Ryan joined them. Even though Steve didn't interact much with Ian (he usually came in the house to say hello and then left to listen to the radio in his car), Ian liked his brother-in-law. Once when Marsha came into the house without Steve, Ian looked at the front door and gestured towards it, clearly asking why her husband had not come in. We all had our own routines, and Ian knew which song, story, or joke belonged to which person. I must admit I did steal one of Steve's jokes since it got such a good reaction from Ian. When I told it, I always gave Steve credit. This is how I related it to Ian: "What does Steve tell you? A man walked into a bar—OUCH!"

ANOTHER INVESTIGATION OF RIVER HOUSE

Since our house is not wheelchair accessible with four steps to the front door and a couple of steep steps to the side door, Ivan typically lifted Ian in the wheelchair up those stairs when he came to visit. Although Ian enjoyed the bump, bump, bump up the stairs, Ivan had strained his shoulder doing that. We requested that Richmond provide some kind of portable ramp that we could set up when Ian visited. Once the ramp was delivered, it allowed us to take Ian in and out of the house as many times as we wanted during a visit. Although Ian missed his "amusement park" ride going up those steps, Ivan did not miss that exertion. There were easier ways to entertain Ian.

In 2008, Ian suffered a fracture of his left hand (cause unknown) along with cellulitis. Fortunately, the break didn't require a cast, since Ian would have gone crazy trying to remove it. However, he continued to suffer from swollen, reddish feet from venous stasis. Although staff were supposed to make sure Ian's feet were elevated when he was sitting in his recliner, too many times I found that not to be the case. Worse than that were the instances when his feet were dangling from his wheelchair because the foot rests were not attached. Besides, he was only supposed to be in that chair for transportation. When we observed those kinds of conditions, Ivan or I reported it to a supervisor.

The year 2008 was an important one in the field of disabilities. The Americans with Disabilities Act was amended to broaden the scope of who should be consider disabled under the law so that a substantial limitation in one major life activity or bodily function qualified an individual as legally disabled. Would that larger umbrella mean more positive attention paid to people like Ian?

At one of our meetings at Richmond, we met Carla, an incredible advocate who was working with Ian's housemate Tom and

     Harriet S. Mosatche

his family. Since each resident was entitled to a Medicaid Service coordinator and the one Ian had been assigned had done far from a stellar job, we asked Carla to take over that position. She visited Ian frequently at his house and at his day program, and he obviously liked Carla as much as we did. She responded to our inquiries and followed up when action was required.

In contrast to the careful attention Carla paid to her responsibilities was the action of the latest River House manager. A new investigation was begun in April 2009 after an anonymous call was made to a Richmond agency administrator with a claim that the "House manager is never around and there is 'neglect' of the residents…". I was pleased that immediate action was taken, and that just a few weeks after the call was made, a full report was provided to family members. The result was that the Manager and the Supervisor were cited for "mistreatment…per 624.4 of the OMRDD Regulations." Specifically,

> *The Manager failed to provide the necessary oversight in the residence by not ensuring the safety of all individuals, adequate supplies and clothing, availability of individuals' personal allowance, recreation completed and documented, adequate training and oversight of staff members, ensuring staff do their jobs as requested and addressing staff issues in an appropriate time frame and manner…Manager did not respond to emails and deadlines and did not have adequate communication with supervisor and staff in the residence. There was a lack of Managerial presence in the residence.*

That last sentence pretty much summed up the problem. As for the house supervisor, she was written up as failing to: ensure that a recreation schedule was in place and documented at completion; provide adequate supervision of staff; create a union-compliant schedule for staff; follow her own work schedule; and communicate adequately with the Residence Manager and staff in the house.

Following those findings in the report was a long list of recommendations ranging from management giving clear direction about when diapers were to be changed to addressing electrical issues in the residence that periodically resulted in a lack of clean towels to having a supervisor present on the night shift to make sure that staff members were awake and alert. Not surprisingly, some staff left (either on their own or at Richmond's request).

Fortunately, Ian was somewhat oblivious to the tension in his house and, even on those occasions when he was neglected, his resilience allowed him to bounce back as soon as someone did something interesting or showed him attention.

MUSIC TO OUR EARS

Among Ian's new Valued Outcomes was one related to participating in music groups. When Ian spent time at our house, we often played CDs for him. I had purchased a three-set CD of "toddler tunes." Ian liked most of the pieces on those CDS, and when he didn't, he grunted to make it clear that the music was not to his liking. Ian had eclectic musical tastes. Ivan had downloaded *American Pie* onto his computer since he knew from hearing Jay sing it to Ian that it was a song that Ian really liked. When Ian came over and wanted to hear that particular song, he pointed to Ivan's computer on his desk in the living room. For other songs, he gestured toward the CD player across the room.

At the beginning of June 2009, a new supervisor arrived at River House. She had been working at another group home, and once again, I was hopeful that she would turn out to be effective and maybe even stay for a while. Almost immediately, I could see the positive difference Natalie made in the house. She was a young, small-boned woman, but she was tough. Not in a mean or unfair way. But she didn't put up with nonsense or excuses from staff, and she held high expectations for Ian and his housemates. Another new staff member was Tara, who was appointed as the interim House Manager. Natalie and Tara shared a heartwarming

     Harriet S. Mosatche

philosophy about working with individuals with developmental disabilities. They showed compassion in dealing with family members as well as residents, focused on the strengths of the residents and staff, and were not afraid to make big changes. Under their efforts, River House was extensively renovated. Walls were painted, new living and dining room furniture was purchased, bathrooms were redone, and what Ian seemed to be happiest about was his new comfortable bed with a colorful quilt and pillow. In an email to Tara and Natalie, with a copy to Richmond's CEO, we described how "ecstatic" we were with the new look of River House. We described the "professionalism and dedication, which went way beyond the call of duty" of the Maintenance Department staff who had crafted headboards for the residents' beds and built-in closets. We noted that, "staff expressed great pride in the place where they spend so much of their time."

Another welcome new addition to River House was a keyboard. Ian and his housemates were the best audience anyone could ask for. I made sure that Ian had the best seat in the house for what became my weekly performances, but Ivan and the staff also moved the others close enough so they could see and hear me. Sometimes staff would sing and dance along. One of the group's favorite songs was "He's Got the Whole World in His Hands." I included each resident's name (sometimes staff, too) in my rendition. When Jessica heard me sing her name, the biggest grin broke out on her face, something that surprised and pleased me since I had never seen her respond so positively and with such understanding to anything before. I sang every verse of the very repetitive "This Old Man" and even played a Russian folk dance song that my piano teacher from decades ago had composed. There were no words, but it had a very lively melody and beat, at least the part that I remembered. "Blue Suede Shoes" was Ian's favorite song, but since I didn't really know the words, I made some of them up. No one cared. Ivan contributed sound effects to, "She'll Be Coming 'Round the Mountain," including loudly snoring at which he was already a pro. Nothing embarrassed us if it made Ian and the other residents happy.

I was a true amateur in the music department, but Elizabeth's boyfriend Evan (she met him in college after she had broken up with Peter) who came with us to River House when they were visiting us during the summer, entertained everyone with his beautiful voice and impeccable piano playing. From the first time I heard Evan speak, I was mesmerized. He was friendly with all the residents and the staff, and they all reacted very positively to him. I thought back to how difficult it had been for me to bring friends home to meet Ian when I was in college. Elizabeth seemed to have no problem at all. Ian was a member of our family, and she wanted her boyfriends to meet him.

WHEELCHAIR WOES

Given all the trauma Ian had endured, the state of his wheelchair might seem minor, but it was where he spent a lot of his time. One thing would be fixed, and another part would break. Ivan wrote detailed emails to staff describing the problems with the chair. For example, in a September 1, 2009 memo, Ivan wrote:

> *When we visited Ian this past weekend, we noticed that the back of Ian's wheelchair was positioned off center, which I think would be somewhat uncomfortable for Ian. The adjustment screws for the seat back were clearly off center (with) the right one showing lots of thread and the left one almost none…I think the staff put our observations in the communication book, so this is just a follow up note to please have someone look at the wheelchair and make the necessary adjustments.*

Other emails described problems with the height of the wheelchair seat. Looking at the copies of the email messages on that topic that went back and forth between Ivan and various Richmond staff, it was evident how long and how much effort it took to get Ian's wheelchair fixed in an optimal way for his safety and comfort.

          Harriet S. Mosatche

While I was sometimes frustrated by Ivan's focus on minutiae, when it came to anything related to Ian, I admired Ivan's straightforward advocacy, perseverance, and attention to detail. When a physical therapist wanted to lower the seat height on Ian's wheelchair, which would enable Ian to propel himself forward, Ivan responded with the equivalent of a legal brief.

He started his letter with: "I am Ian Rosenberg's brother-in-law and advocate." He went on to state:

> *I disagree strongly with the conclusion in your email... that the seat height on Ian's wheelchair should be lowered because he propels the wheelchair with his feet and needs a lower height to do so efficiently... We have never seen Ian move his wheelchair forward, only backward. Moving backward is dangerous since he does not, and probably cannot, turn his head to see where he is going, and he could back into a position where he could harm himself or another... He could perhaps even tip the wheelchair backwards.*

Later in the email, Ivan wrote:

> *I believe that it is cost efficient and more beneficial for Ian's comfort, health and safety if the seat is higher so that his feet can rest more comfortably on the footrest and so that he will have much less leverage when he pushes against the footrest. I do not believe that the ability to propel himself backward in the wheelchair should be viewed in any sense as a countervailing benefit.*

Since the seat back of Ian's wheelchair had still not been correctly adjusted, Ivan also made the following request in this email:

> *...The seat back is not centered properly. The center of the seat back is left of center of the wheelchair as a whole. The*

*seat back seems to have an adjustment mechanism for
centering, but no one has adjusted it. Ian therefore has to
seat himself in an uncomfortable position in the wheelchair.
I have complained about this for several months both
verbally and by email. I would appreciate it if you would
issue the appropriate directions to deal with this problem
immediately.*

The physical therapist agreed to our request and the wheelchair
was finally overhauled. Since we had been invited to attend the
Wheelchair Clinic with Ian, we participated and made sure that
the changes in his chair were the ones that would be best for Ian.
By that time, we had become experts in the physics of wheelchairs.
It had taken several months of ceaseless advocacy, but the result
was well worth it.

 Harriet S. Mosatche

CHAPTER 29

Promises, Frustrations, and Finally, Improvements

n November of 2009, Marsha became a grandmother when my niece Sherry gave birth to a healthy baby girl. I was excited to be a great-aunt, but I knew I would be paying close attention to how Abigail developed, just to make sure everything was fine. I didn't share my concerns with anyone since they weren't particularly rational. Since Ian loved babies, I told him about Abigail and assured him that he would have an opportunity to meet his great-niece soon. Ian reacted by pulling up his shirt, showing his stomach. "Yes, Abigail is a baby," I responded.

PERSON-CENTERED PLANNING

In October 2009, the families received a letter from Richmond informing us that Derrick, with eight years of experience in the field, had assumed the duties of Manager at River House. He seemed nice enough when I met him, and Ian liked the tattoos inked on Derrick's upper arms. "So you'd like a tattoo, like the one Derrick has?" I asked Ian, who responded by pulling up the sleeve of his shirt and grinning.

Tara initiated a new process for all the residents of River House, something officially called "Person-Centered Planning." In the first phase of this process, staff and family members, working together, came up with a plan design to "find out who Ian is and create a better lifestyle" for him. Then, just as I was feeling comfortable with the work that the managers at River House were doing, I learned that Tara would be leaving to take on a position at Richmond with greater responsibility. Although I understood why she was needed in that other job, I was disheartened by the news. Under Tara and Natalie, Ian's home had been functioning much better than at any other time. While Tara assured me that her replacement would be great, I had seen enough supervisors at River House to know how difficult it would be to find someone who could both motivate staff and keep the residents happy. I feared that the rollercoaster was headed downward.

Since a good speech and language therapist could help Ian learn more effective ways to communicate, Ivan and I ceaselessly advocated for Ian to receive this form of help. Suddenly, from not getting any speech therapy for years, Ian was receiving therapy from two different people, one from Richmond and one from an outside agency. Ironically, the two speech and language therapists weren't communicating with each other, which could be confusing to Ian. When I met Aaron, the Richmond speech-language therapist assigned to Ian, I was impressed by his openness to our suggestions and his knowledge of strategies that he could use with Ian. In a letter to Ivan, he wrote: "…Ian exhibited a favorable score and prognosis for therapy was good." Aaron turned out to be not only a great speech therapist for Ian, but also one of his most significant allies. Ivan and I wrote a letter of commendation for Aaron that led to his receiving a well-deserved staff recognition award.

The second part of Person-Center Planning for Ian took place during the winter of 2010, and the outcome was a detailed chart for and about Ian:

- Attributes and Talents (ranging from "recognizes something new" to "good sense of humor")
- Interests and Hobbies (such as "loves foreign accents and slapstick comedy")

     Harriet S. Mosatche

- Supports Needed or Desired (including speech therapy, getting attention, and family)
- Preferences and Priorities (ranging from his "preference for certain staff" to "loves to be praised" as a form of motivation)
- Resources and Networks (including visits to the New York Botanical Garden and book stores)
- Community Connections (ranging from pet therapists to visiting his family and the library)

A Communication Chart was also developed with three columns: Ian Does This, We Think It Means, and We Should. One example was: When Ian grunts, that either means that he has to use the bathroom or does not like what he is doing, and staff should investigate whether he needs to be changed or he wants a change in the activity he is engaged in. Another example is when Ian touches different parts of his body that means that he recognizes something "new" (perhaps a haircut or eyeglasses), and staff should praise him for his awareness or efforts.

The final part of the framework was labeled "Action Planning." The five columns were:

- Things I am interested in/want to explore
- Places that support my interest
- What to do next—specific steps
- People who will help
- By when

One of the items listed for things Ian is interested in was: "Starting a book collection." Places that were listed to support that interest were Barnes and Noble, Target, and (the now defunct) Borders. The specific step described in the plan was to create a schedule and put a plan in place. The people who were listed as helping Ian take this action were River House and Ian's family with the deadline given as two weeks.

Ian's February 2010 report described six valued outcomes, ranging from "Ian would like to assist in drying himself after his shower" and "Ian would like to play the keyboard." The report included information from the Person-Centered Planning and noted that Ian would be working on three different areas: communication, starting a book collection, and community outings related to music with the residence and day program implementing those actions.

THEY KEEP COMING AND GOING

While Derrick, as House Manager, seemed pleasant enough, he was no substitute for Tara. Even though Natalie reported to Derrick, she was the one who made the house function well. After a brief investigation of an incident involving a staff member who was reported to have been loud and abusive in communicating with his co-workers in front of the residents of River House, that individual was quickly removed from the house. By May, Derrick was gone as well, which was definitely not a loss. He was rarely around anyway, and it turned out that he had taken on a second job for another agency. He always had an excuse for not responding to phone calls or emails, such as illness, training courses, or meetings. One weekend when he was supposed to be on call, he never responded to urgent messages left on his phone. That was the last straw for the administration.

While I was relieved that Derrick was no longer at River House, I was outraged when I learned soon afterwards that Natalie had been removed as supervisor and offered a non-supervisory position elsewhere in the agency. Ivan discovered, by his persistent questioning, that complaints had been lodged against her by staff at the house, but that the residents had not been harmed in any way. Ivan and I prepared a four-page letter to the Richmond CEO detailing why we thought Natalie needed to be reinstated. We included information about the succession of terrible supervisors and managers who rarely left their basement office, allowed the staff to abuse the residents, or lied about taking care of matters but neglecting to

     Harriet S. Mosatche

follow through. Tara and Natalie were the exceptions. When Ivan reached Natalie at home, it was clear that she was as distraught as we were about what had happened to her. Ian had responded to her very positively, she knew what was going on at River House, and she had worked with us to do what seemed impossible (including going against bureaucracy to obtain a second speech evaluation). Tom's family felt exactly as we did, and they, too, weren't going to accept Natalie's departure without a fight. In our letter, we wrote (among many other things) that:

> …once Tara left and Derrick took over as manager in name but failed to take any active role in managing the house, Natalie was left out to dry without any managerial support. The staff tried to go back to their old ways where they ran the house as they saw fit and resented Natalie's insistence that they care for the residents properly.

We further suggested that,

> …even if there were, in fact, any legitimate issues about Natalie's supervisory style, then Richmond should have provided some coaching or mediation, rather than removing such a dedicated employee from her position.

Unfortunately, our advocacy did not help Natalie get her job back at River House, and in June, families received yet another letter letting us know that a new person had been hired. I liked Fran as soon as I met her, but I was skeptical. Derrick, Kathleen, Martha, and John had all been friendly, said all the right things about working with and caring for people with developmental disabilities, and then had disappointed us, and more important had let down the residents of River House. When the families were invited to talk with Fran, many of us said the same thing. We would wait and see. Since I am typically an optimist, I thought that maybe she would be different, the one who could turn things around. Ivan and I decided we should make more of our visits a surprise to staff so we could see what was really going on.

DISTRESSING VISITS

On a Sunday afternoon visit to River House soon after Fran had been appointed to the position of house manager, but before she officially started, we arrived without calling first. While Ivan parked the car, Elizabeth and I went to the door and rang the doorbell. Carl, one of the aides, opened the door, and I saw that Ian was sitting in his wheelchair, which had no footrests attached. He was wearing a very wet t-shirt and his feet, purple and very cold, were dangling. While I went to get a fresh shirt for Ian along with shoes and socks so we could take him out, Ivan asked why Ian was not sitting in his recliner, which is where he should have been to keep his legs elevated. Carl said that Ian's footrests had been left at the day program, that as soon as the doorbell rang, he moved Ian into the wheelchair so he could be ready to go outside. I knew that his explanation was not credible since there wasn't time for that to happen between the ringing of the doorbell and the opening of the door. Besides, Ian's legs would not have been so cold and discolored if he had just been put into the wheelchair. Ivan wrote to Fran's supervisor and copied Fran describing the situation with Ian, but also mentioning the fact that the aides were not interacting with any of the residents.

When Fran officially took over as house manager, we met with her and other members of the day program and house staff to discuss Ian's care. Fran quickly followed up that meeting by telling us that she would be purchasing a bean bag chair, a CD player, interactive gadgets for Ian to play with, and pillows and wedges for positioning at the day program. We also suggested that she get a "bobo doll," a plastic air-filled doll that is weighted on the curved bottom and bounces back when hit. I remembered Ian playing with one when he was home. Upon doing further research, Ivan found that the current term was "bop bags," and one was ordered for Ian.

    Harriet S. Mosatche

While we waited to see whether Fran would be able to change the atmosphere at River House, Ivan kept in touch with Tom's sister so we could present a consistent message about what our loved ones needed and about problems that needed to be addressed at their home. Tom's sister, Georgia, wrote about her parents visiting River House when only one staff member was present. When they inquired about the others who were supposed to be on duty, they were told that the others were on break. But no one else appeared in the more than one hour of her parents' visit. She also told Ivan that Ian was in his wheelchair during that entire time. The minimum staffing ratio was four to one, and two staff should not be on break at the same time. There would be no honeymoon period for Fran. She would quickly be receiving emails from Tom and Ian's families.

After our visit on July 4th, Ivan wrote another email to Fran. Ian was sitting in his recliner with the footrest up—yay! But the workers were barely civil, giving us a begrudging hello in response to our greeting. The television was playing some kind of drama at a very loud volume, with a man and woman yelling at each other. Jessica was right in front of the television with her back to the set, so the program was certainly not for her benefit. Alice, Alex, and Susan were at the dining room table eating dinner. When Ivan asked for the remote so he could lower the volume, one staff said it was lost, while another one found it and turned the television off. When we returned to the living room after spending time with Ian in his room, the television was back on with the same couple yelling at each other—loud enough to drown out whatever noises the residents made. Again, the staff paused the show, and we left. Fran wrote back explaining that she was spending time at River House during the evening meal and "role modeling" more appropriate social behaviors. She asked for more time to work closely with staff and noted that they are dedicated to the well-being of the residents.

The following weekend, we went to River House twice. Since Ian's recreation schedule indicated he was going shopping and out to dinner on Saturday, we arrived early in the afternoon. We had picked up my brother Jay and greeted Alex, Susan, and Alice, assuming that Ian was in his room being changed. I gave Susan a new *O* magazine and Ivan and Alex played together with the bop bag. After a few minutes Ivan asked whether Ian was being changed and when he would be ready to go out. The staff member said that Ian wasn't at home and that he had gone out to eat. When Ivan asked when Ian would be home, the response was a curt, "I don't know." We then left. The staff could have told us when we walked in that Ian wasn't there but they didn't bother.

We returned on Sunday afternoon at 4:30, and we saw the staff moving the residents to the table for dinner. The television was on at a normal volume, showing some kind of domestic drama. The staff were unfriendly and basically ignored us. We asked if Ian could eat later so we could take Ian out to the patio for a while. No one could locate the key for the elevator lift, which would have allowed us to easily take Ian out to the patio for our visit. It was a shame that almost the only time the patio was used was when there was an official party, even though it was a lovely setting for family visits.

Time for another of Ivan's letters to Fran, explaining that the only time in the past few weeks that our visits to Ian had been pleasant were when she or a supervisor from another house was present. "That has to change," Ivan wrote. Ivan's final sentence in that email was:

> *While we are willing to let bygones be bygones if we see a change in the attitude and behavior of the staff in taking care of the residents, we will not permit bad conduct to continue without making an issue of it.*

FINALLY, SOME POSITIVE CHANGES

We were not convinced that Fran recognized what she was up against. However, it didn't take too long for her to make us into believers. She was honest about what she could do (and what she couldn't) and the timeframe for taking action. While she supported

     Harriet S. Mosatche

her staff, she made it clear that River House belonged to Ian, Tom, Alex, Susan, Alice, and Jessica. That was a philosophy that resonated with me. Since we had written so many complaint letters to Fran, we felt it was important to describe the positive changes we had recently noticed in the house. In a July 24th email, Ivan wrote:

> *The staff inside the house, Debby and Bettina, were very friendly and helpful. Both of them greeted us on our arrival in a welcoming manner…Later when we returned, Debby immediately got Ian a glass of water…and when Harriet played the keyboard for the residents, Debby engaged the other residents present…and helped Jessica with the Hokey Pokey when Harriet played that song. All in all, it was a very pleasant visit.*

Meanwhile, in another part of my life, my consulting business was going well with evaluation projects, some grant writing, program development, and executive coaching. I now had both Robert and Elizabeth involved in answering questions for my online advice column. I like to think that their myriad experiences with Ian helped them develop their empathy, which they used in answering questions. From time to time, I traveled on business, but these trips were never more than three or four days, so I was still able to keep up with visiting Ian on a regular basis. Ivan was busy taking care of legal matters for a few clients, but spent much more of his time taking care of family issues, including all aspects of Ian's welfare and also the financial and legal matters of his parents who had moved from New York to Ohio at the end of 2009.

Elizabeth had graduated from college that May and decided to move back home until she found a job. She broke up with her boyfriend. Ian and I would both miss Evan's beautiful voice, but Elizabeth had thought long and hard about what was right for her, and I admired that. Eventually, she wanted to earn a Ph.D. in psychology, but after being rejected from doctoral programs the first time around, she realized that she needed to gain more research experience in the field so she started looking for that kind of work. Since she was living at home, she began to visit Ian regularly once again. I watched with pride as my daughter showed compassion and patience. She had come so far from the little girl who kept her distance from Ian, who didn't know what to say or do with him. She was now a confident young woman. When I asked Ian where Dr. Lawner was, he pointed right at Elizabeth. Yes, that title was premature, but Ian liked the question and Elizabeth appreciated my confidence in her.

That summer, Robert spent six weeks exploring southeast Asia, after leaving his marketing job at a law firm. He planned to start law school in California in August. Before he left on his Asian adventure and when he returned to New York after the trip, he spent time with Ian. By that time, Robert had embellished the Willie Dreshen story further by adding his friends who had become teachers. Like all the other teachers in the story, they told Willie Dreshen that he needed an operation. And each time Robert told the story, he ended with a different twist—Willie Dreshen decided to go to law school although he knew his nasal voice might not go over well with a jury or Willie Dreshen became a teacher and recommended operations to many of his students.

Ivan's parents had given up their car before moving to Ohio (we had asked them to stop driving years before because of their visual impairments) so Robert had a car to move him and his stuff across the country. He asked a girl he had started seeing before he left for Asia to accompany him on this road trip. To my surprise, since she hardly knew him, Kaleigh said yes. She planned to help him settle into his new life on the west coast and return to New York in time for the classes she was taking toward her graduate degree in speech and language pathology. The future seemed bright for all of us.

			Harriet S. Mosatche

CHAPTER 30

Decisions

Robert and Kaleigh were on their way to California when we received an email from Fran on a Saturday in mid-August telling us that over the past couple of weeks Ian had vomited his meal a few times. One of his housemates had been ill with some kind of stomach bug, so it didn't seem to be a big deal.

UPSETTING INFORMATION

On the following Monday, River House staff noticed that Ian had some swelling and a bruise on his right ear, and on Tuesday, he had been sent home from the day program when they noticed that his lips were pale and he was rubbing his stomach excessively. When Fran noticed that he looked pale, Ian was taken to the doctor to have blood drawn. When I received the email with all these details, I mainly felt relieved that staff were so attentive to Ian's health, but not really worried. When I visited with Ian that weekend, he seemed cheerful and fit.

The following week, Fran emailed us again to let us know that Ian's blood tests results concerned his doctor enough so that he referred Ian for an appointment with a nephrologist, a kidney specialist. It didn't seem urgent since that appointment was scheduled for mid-October, two months away. However, since Mom had died of end-stage renal disease, we asked if the nephrologist could move the appointment up. We had become huge fans of Fran since the atmosphere at the house had changed dramatically—from toxic to welcoming and helpful. When we arrived for a visit, staff were friendly with us and the residents. One staff member might be joking with Tom while another was polishing Jessica's nails.

The results of Ian's renal ultrasound done on August 23rd indicated "bilateral renal atrophy" and "altered renal cortical echogenicity suggestive of medical renal disease." I tried not to panic, but I knew the news wasn't good. Further tests had to be done, so Ian was hospitalized for a couple of days. Since he kept pulling out the tubes and disconnecting wires, he was restrained in his hospital bed. I tried to put on a happy face to prevent Ian from seeing my despair when I entered his hospital room and saw his hands and legs tied to the sides of his bed. I told a nurse I would prevent him from pulling anything out if I could remove or at least loosen the restraints. Ian hugged me with obvious gratitude. Fran later told us she did the same thing when she visited him. I liked her even more then. Ivan told the Willie Dreshen story, and we went through a number of other routines and songs for him. When Ian was back home, he resumed his regular routine, which included going to his day program.

On September 7th, I received a fax from Ian's nephrologist detailing the results of all the tests. This chilling sentence stood out: "The renal atrophy noted on the sonogram suggests a chronic process and usually indicates that significant renal recovery is not expected." The one recommendation in the report was to increase fluid intake. Now I wondered whether Ian's long-time desire to drink copious amounts of water was his body's attempt to keep his kidney functioning at a more optimum level. The report also included some possible causes, such as a congenital defect, hypertension, or drug-induced renal toxicity. I'm not a physician, but my thinking was that a familial predisposition to kidney disorders and years of high-dosage Dilantin (prescribed to prevent seizures) and other drugs might be the basis for what was happening to Ian right now.

     Harriet S. Mosatche

IMPORTANT CONVERSATIONS

I needed to know as much as possible about Ian's present condition as well as his prognosis. I talked to Marsha about what I had learned and asked her to talk to her family and our brother Jay, who I knew would be devastated since he had long thought of Ian as his best friend and the most significant person in his life. Ivan and I talked to our children, Robert by telephone and Elizabeth in person. Robert wanted to know about treatment options. Elizabeth immediately went on the Internet to gather information and also contacted a college friend who was just beginning medical school. She asked whether she should be tested to see if she could be a match for Ian, allowing her to donate a kidney to him. While I was moved by her compassion and generosity, I told her that with our family medical history she'd better hold on to both of her kidneys. Besides, Ian was hardly a viable candidate for a transplant.

Ivan and I spoke by telephone to the nephrologist, a very kind and patient doctor. He answered our questions and made recommendations, even one I was not yet ready to consider: that when Ian's condition worsened, as it would, that he not be put through dialysis or placed on a list for a transplant. For both of those courses of action, a high level of motivation and understanding was required. Ian, who couldn't stand a long-sleeved shirt or gloves, would not tolerate the restrictions that would be part of dialysis. Marsha and I did a lot of talking. And we cried together, too. Neither of us could imagine life without Ian. Ivan and I discussed what would be best for Ian. Ivan emphasized that Ian would have to be sedated and restrained every time he was dialyzed, which would need to take place at least three times weekly for several hours each time. Doctors had always found it hard to knock Ian out for dental procedures. It's as if his brain fought against sedation. A fistula or tube that would have to be inserted for the dialysis would become a constant annoyance for Ian. He would definitely work at getting that irritant away from his body. And putting that in required surgery. We asked ourselves: What quality of life would Ian have?

Hadn't he suffered enough in his 51 years? Were we trying to keep him alive for us? What would Ian want?

Ian's doctors told us that he needed to drink at least two liters of water daily. That meant eight eight-ounce glasses of water. I knew that he could do that. His condition was called diabetes insipidus, which occurs when the kidneys are unable to conserve water as they filter the blood. Maybe I should have pushed for medical tests years earlier when every report on Ian described how much water he drank. Or maybe blood testing done in the last ten years should have been flagged by medical personnel for further investigation. But it was too late to do that kind of second-guessing. We had to deal with Ian's condition as it was right now. And his doctors made it clear that it was terminal. I was heartbroken. My 51 year old brother was dying. But he was more than a brother. He was my baby, and I was his favorite person in the whole world.

     Harriet S. Mosatche

TIME FOR HARD DECISIONS

On October 11, 2010, Ivan and I attended a special team meeting to discuss hospice planning for Ian. A social worker from Phelps Hospice, part of a well-known hospital in our county, attended the meeting along with several Richmond administrators. Everyone was very kind to me. I stayed composed although tears welled up in my eyes and my voice cracked a bit as I explained what our family wanted for Ian. Our main concern was that Ian be kept free of pain. The social worker asked about a DNR order, which we had not yet put in place. Everything was happening so quickly. Barely a month had gone by since I first learned of Ian's diagnosis, and here we were at a meeting discussing not resuscitating him if and when he went into cardiac arrest. I also requested that Ian remain in his home at River House as long as possible. Richmond administrators, whom we had fought with in the past, bent over backwards to follow my wishes. They said that if Ian got to a point where he needed 24 hour nursing care, he could be transferred to the main building. Fran suggested that staff from River House could be assigned to his care. I liked the idea that he would be surrounded by people who knew and cared about him.

Soon after that meeting, Fran wrote a touching email to Ivan and me, in which she said: "I would like to let you both know how impressed I am by your love, commitment, and advocacy of Ian. He is a fortunate man. I have grown fond of him and both of you as well."

I thanked Fran for her email and then wrote:

Ian has always been very special to me, and his disability was the reason I decided to become a psychologist. Since Ivan joined our family, he has thought of Ian as a brother and has treated him that way. Ivan and I both judge people by the way they interact with Ian—it's a simple way to see who is decent and caring. You have passed the "test" with flying colors and so have many of the staff. We are deeply appreciative of everything you are doing for Ian and how you are helping to make the process of slowly losing Ian more bearable. We will continue to rely on you, the River House and Richmond staff, and the Hospice personnel in the difficult time ahead of us. Ian cannot thank you, but I know he is grateful, too, for the loving care he receives.

What a long way we had all come from the days at BDC.

That October, Elizabeth moved to Washington, DC, where she had landed a great job as a research assistant for a research and policy organization. Although it wasn't easy for her to move away from home with everything that was going on with Ian, I assured her that she could not pass up such a wonderful career opportunity and that she could talk to Ian on Skype. Living at home over the summer had allowed Elizabeth and Ian to grow very close since they saw each other weekly, and she understood that he didn't have a lot of time left. She planned to visit often, and she did.

I wanted the families of Ian's housemates to be told about his condition, but asked that they not discuss Ian's illness with him. I wanted his remaining time to be as normal as possible, including attending his day program as long as he could. I was not going to tell Ian he was dying since it would serve no purpose. We were going to make sure that Ian's life would be filled with as much joy as possible. No one knew how much time he had left, but it would be measured in months and not years. Sabine, the River House supervisor whom Fran had hired, knowing how much Ian loved Elvis Presley found a venue that she knew he would love and made sure he experienced an outing there. Afterwards, Sabine emailed us to say that, "Ian had a blast…He was all smiles as he watched numerous Elvis impersonators. He consumed all of his food including dessert." One of the best email messages I had ever received.

PAPERWORK AMIDST EMOTIONAL TURMOIL

Ivan worked with Richmond to learn the regulations and protocol for obtaining a DNR for Ian, a prerequisite for him receiving hospice care. I wanted every possible service for Ian. That would include an aide for four hours a day and regular visits from a nurse. When the hospice social worker asked if we wanted to schedule time with their chaplain, I readily agreed. We met her the first time at River House. My friend Diane asked if she could join us for that visit, not because she wanted to meet the chaplain, but because she had long wanted to meet the brother I had talked about for years. What Diane didn't say was that she wanted to meet Ian before it was too late. Although Ian was happy to see me, he seemed agitated during that visit. Ivan and I tried to soothe him with songs and stories, but they just weren't working. I had already been told that agitation is one of the signs of deteriorating kidney function as toxins stay in the body. The hospice chaplain, Rabbi Jo, talked with Ian and us for a little while and then asked if we wanted her to pray with Ian. "Yes, I would like that," I said, although I am not a religious person. When she asked if her prayer should be in English or Hebrew, I suggested the latter. Jo took Ian's hand and began to pray in Hebrew, including using Ian's Hebrew name. Ian's demeanor immediately changed. The agitation was replaced by calm, a deep and peaceful calm that seemed like a miracle.

It turned out that the regulations for the issuance of DNR orders for those with developmental disabilities were contained in the Health Care Decisions Act, which had been amended in June 2010. Step one was the identification of an appropriate surrogate. As an "actively involved adult sibling," I fit the bill. Step two required that the surrogate make the decision to withhold or withdraw life-saving treatment and that the decision be given orally or in writing to the patient's attending physician. I signed the paperwork. It sounds so simple, but the reality was that signing the form indicating that Ian would not be given possibly life-saving dialysis came only after heart-wrenching discussions with Ivan, Marsha, and Jay. The third step required the confirmation of the lack of capacity of the individual to make health care decisions. Ian's doctor and an independent psychologist took care of that piece.

Three other steps rounded out the requirements to withhold or withdraw life-sustaining treatment (LST). Two doctors had to agree that Ian had a terminal condition *and* that LST would "impose an extraordinary burden on the individual." Unfortunately, Ian met those two conditions easily. Notification to the individual was required, but the Act allowed "a therapeutic exception." All agreed that it would serve no purpose to tell Ian what was *not* going to happen. Once all the requirements were met, which involved a cast of dozens, from attorneys to agency and state administrators to doctors, the DNR order was put into effect. Renewal was required every 90 days. I hoped for many renewals.

MAKING THE MOST OF OUR TIME

The new routine for Ian was attendance at his day program and then four hours with a special hospice aide in the evening. Ivan and I visited on the second day that the aide showed up. She was far from ideal. Actually, she didn't even meet the criterion of mediocre. He needed "warm and caring." What he got was "cold and indifferent." What she wanted in a patient was someone who needed only passive care. Ivan called the agency the next morning and said not only was this woman not appropriate for Ian, but she shouldn't be assigned to anyone. The hospice agency quickly found a substitute, one who turned out to be exactly what I wanted for Ian. Kenisha was kind and attentive, and Ian liked her. Of course, when we showed up for visits in the evening, he did indicate to Kenisha that she needed to leave us alone.

Once Ian was diagnosed, all of us started visiting him more frequently. Marsha and Steve, sometimes with their son Ryan, drove from Connecticut to see Ian every weekend. Marsha's grandchild, Abigail, met Ian before she turned a year old. Sherry and Jeff brought her to our house when Ian was visiting, and they were equally intrigued by each other. Abigail waved to Ian, and he clapped his hands. While I played and sang the Hokey Pokey, Ian rubbed his ears and Abigail moved in time to the music—a Norman Rockwell

    Harriet S. Mosatche

moment. When I asked Ian on subsequent visits what he did when he saw Abigail, he grinned and clapped his hands. They had made a quick and special connection.

On most three-day holiday weekends, Elizabeth took the bus up from Washington, DC, to New York so she could visit Ian. Since Robert was in school in California, he talked to Ian by phone or on Skype. Once when Ian was at our house on a visit, Ivan brought his laptop down to the floor when he was able to reach Robert on Skype. Usually Ian got very excited hearing Robert's voice, but on this day, Ian was being entertained by Jay and me and he didn't pay much attention to the computer. "Focus, focus, Ian," my husband said. I didn't think Ian understood that word, but something about Ivan's insistent "focus, focus" made him smile and made Jay and me laugh. I had a new routine now for Ian, imitating Ivan urging Ian to focus on the computer screen.

In most ways, Ian seemed the same as ever. The impish grin, the attention to differences in his environment, the joy he showed when I visited, the grunting when he disliked a particular song. But there was one evident change. Ian no longer laughed aloud. He smiled a lot, but the loud guffaws that made me laugh along with him were absent. Maybe he was getting weaker—from the toxins accumulating in his body, from the painkillers he was given when he seemed to be suffering. I wished I could hear his laughter again, but I would have to settle for a genuine grin.

When we wanted updates about Ian from Fran, we talked in the River House basement. I didn't want Ian or his housemates to hear those conversations. In late November, Carolyn, one of the staff who often cared for Ian, came down to the basement while we were talking with Fran and gave me a hug. I walked upstairs with her while Ivan continued his discussion with Fran. "Ian is going to be okay," she said.

"His birthday is coming up in a month. I want Ian to be around for that," I told her.

"He's going to be fine," Carolyn responded. "He's not going to die. He's doing great. I won't let anything happen to Papa." That was the nickname she had given to Ian. I stayed composed as I sang and talked with Ian, but when I called Marsha later on to tell her what Carolyn had said and how much she obviously cared for our brother, the tears came. Ian was finally in a wonderful place cared for by dedicated people who loved him, and he was going to die, no matter what Carolyn said. Fran told us that many of the staff were having a tough time accepting the facts of Ian's illness, and that she had sought counseling for them. Ian finally had gained the love and support that I had always wanted for him. How bittersweet.

In 2010, Rosa's Law was passed, which changed references in many federal statutes from "mental retardation" to "intellectual disability."

 Harriet S. Mosatche

CHAPTER 31

Dayenu—Enough is Enough

We had a 52nd birthday party for Ian in December 2010 at River House with lots of food, music, and laughter. It was hard not to think that the odds of Ian reaching his 53rd birthday were extremely slim.

GOOD DAYS AND BAD

Ian had good days and bad ones. On good days, he spent all day at his program, ate dinner with Kenisha's help, and went on shopping trips. On bad days, he refused one or more of his meals, went home early from his program, and slept a lot. I saw him on both kinds of days. On his bad days, I just had to work a little bit harder to make Ian smile. A hospice nurse visited weekly, and with his reports to Ian's doctor, the medication was adjusted. When he began to choke while drinking water, his speech-language pathologist Aaron advised that his drinks be thickened to make it easier for him to swallow. River House used a powdered thickening agent. I found something better— thick juice drinks, which Ian liked. We always kept a couple at our house and each week brought a supply over for Ian's house.

In January, my husband Ivan went to the doctor for his annual physical. He felt fine, but his PSA was elevated from the previous year and that had been higher than the year before. After a visit to his urologist followed by a biopsy, and other tests, the diagnosis was prostate cancer. Fortunately, it was contained within that organ.

Because the cancer showed up in numerous sites on the prostate, he didn't have too many choices regarding treatment. He was scheduled for robotic surgery in March, but before that he needed pre-op clearance. I just wanted the surgery to be over, to get that cancer out of Ivan's body. Meanwhile, we continued to visit Ian three times a week, and while his spirits remained high, he was beginning to look gaunt and sometimes refused a meal or even his favorite juice drink.

In February, on one of my visits to Ian, I called Marsha, so he could hear her tell him her Jimmy story. Marsha did not sound good, and she said she didn't want to talk to me while I was visiting Ian, but Sherry was having problems. I learned that Sherry was so overwhelmed by everything that was going on in her life—the death of her grandmother (Marsha's mother-in-law) while she was in labor with Abigail, being let go from the teaching job she loved, Ian's terminal illness, and the adjustment to the demands of motherhood—that she began to withdraw a bit from reality. It was easier for her to believe that Ian wasn't dying than to face another death of someone she loved.

Ivan's pre-op clearance in March turned out to be less routine than expected. A factor showed up in his blood that required him to see a hematologist for further tests. His surgeon needed to know whether special precautions would be necessary either before or after the scheduled operation. Although I understood the reason for the delay, it was one more thing to deal with, and I was nearing my limit.

BAD DAYS AND WORSE ONES

At the end of March, we met with Rabbi Jo and Sara (the hospice social worker) at River House one morning. I spent a little time with Ian before he left for his day program and then Rabbi Jo asked me what she should pray for. I had begun to really look forward to praying with the chaplain. With what was going on with Ian, Ivan, and Sherry, I asked that no more bad things happen in our family.

    Harriet S. Mosatche

The prayer contained the Hebrew word "Dayenu," which I understood from the many years of singing Dayenu at Passover seders as meaning "It is (would have been) enough."

Dayenu was not in the cards for us quite yet. That Wednesday, while walking with my friend and neighbor Judy, whom I had walked with hundreds of times before, Judy began having an allergic reaction from something she had eaten for lunch. As hives flared up all over, we started to walk back home. She said she just needed to take Benadryl, which she had in her medicine cabinet, and would be fine. I called Ivan to pick us up so we could get her home quickly. By the time Ivan arrived, Judy was on the ground, and I called 911. I helped Judy into the car just as she collapsed, and realized that my friend was in anaphylactic shock. The ambulance arrived quickly, put Judy on a stretcher, and we followed them to the hospital, calling her husband on the way. After a stay in the hospital, we never walked again without an epinephrine pen, which I learned how to administer.

That Friday, Elizabeth called Ivan's cell phone at nine in the morning, and said in as cheery a voice as she could muster: "Hi Dad. Don't freak out. I'm okay, but I am in the ER at a hospital. A car ran over my foot when I was crossing the street, and I was taken here by ambulance." Hearing that conversation, my heart began to race. Fortunately, no bones were broken, and other than a very swollen foot and ankle, some contusions, and a badly scraped handbag holding a now- smashed iPod and water bottle, damaged by the car mirror hitting her bag as she fell to the ground, she was okay. Shaken up and vowing never to use that particular crosswalk again, Elizabeth was going to be fine.

Just a week later, on Thursday night, April 7th, I had a severe asthma attack. I had not had one in years, but I always had my emergency inhaler available and used it. The next morning, I did some work on the computer and worked out at the gym. Those 45 minutes on the elliptical machine had been a great source of stress relief, although I hadn't seen any changes to my weight. After lunch I took a nap, and when I woke up I noticed that my lisp was a bit more pronounced. "I must have bitten my tongue," I thought. Ivan didn't say anything so it was probably nothing. Before going to Costco to purchase more of Ian's special juice and other items, I stopped by at Judy's to see if she wanted anything. She didn't say anything about my speech.

The next morning, my speech still seemed a bit abnormal, and I was making more mistakes when using my Blackberry with my left hand. I told Ivan that maybe I should go to the doctor. Since my doctor wasn't in, I was scheduled to see the covering physician at 4:30 that afternoon. After checking my blood pressure, which was very high, he suggested that I go to the hospital. Friday night is not a good time to be in an emergency room. I was admitted to the hospital sometime in the middle of the night. I knew that if I had had a stroke, it was too late to receive the drug that could undo any damage that had occurred. Throughout the weekend, I was monitored and tested, but it wasn't until Sunday afternoon—my 62nd birthday—that the neurologist told me that I had suffered a stroke. When I explained that the extraordinary amount of stress I had been under in the past few weeks might have contributed to the stroke, he made it clear he didn't want any details and dismissed me with, "Just don't let those little arguments with your husband get to you" If only little fights with my husband had been the source of my stress. I felt like punching the doctor.

WE CAN STILL LAUGH

Ivan was scheduled for robotic surgery to remove his prostate on Tuesday, April 12th, at noon. I was hoping to be discharged in time to see Ivan before his surgery. At least we were in the same hospital although in very different areas. As soon as the doctor signed the appropriate forms and a nurse explained them to me, I headed down to the surgery unit and was able to talk to Ivan for a few minutes.

    Harriet S. Mosatche

My cousin Rona and my friend Cindy kept me company while I waited for the operation to be over. When fire alarm bells sounded, I was not surprised—just more drama for my not very calm life. After a couple of hours, Ivan's doctor came out to say that the surgery had gone well. I couldn't help but notice that the doctor had a bruised black eye, something that I hadn't seen before the surgery. By now, I was giddy, and so were Cindy and Rona. My friend Diane also showed up at the hospital, and we brainstormed what might have caused the black eye. Had Ivan punched the doctor while under anesthesia? Had the robotic arm gotten out of control? Had a nurse thrown something at the doctor when he said something fresh? When the doctor made his rounds at the hospital a couple of days later, Ivan inquired about the cause of the black eye. "It was from a disgruntled patient," the doctor joked. Or at least we hoped he was joking.

Ivan came home from the hospital on Friday, April 15th, and that weekend, we arranged to have Ian come over to visit. Neither Ivan nor I were in any shape to take care of Ian on our own, both of us still recovering from our medical issues. But we didn't want to miss seeing him since it was becoming more obvious that Ian's health was on a downward path, although he still managed to rally, sometimes for days at a time. Elizabeth and Robert were both in town that weekend and entertained Ian with stories, songs, and dances. Robert's girlfriend Kaleigh won my heart when she touched Ian's leg as she said goodbye to him. After years of people being afraid to be near my brother, here was someone who showed him total acceptance.

That day, Marsha and her family also came over with Abigail. She and Ian connected with waves, smiles, and clapping hands. I played all of Ian's favorite songs, and Marsha made Ian her famous tuna fish sandwich. Even when he didn't want anything else, he gobbled up Marsha's tuna sandwich. She began to bring it with her when she visited Ian at his house. The following Saturday, April 23rd, Ivan woke up with a sore throat and decided it was too risky to expose Ian to any possible infection, so Marsha and Steve picked me up on their way to visit Ian. Fran arranged a "day on the town" that coming week for Ian and Tom. Instead of spending the day at the program, they would shop for new clothes and eat at a restaurant. It all seemed so normal.

THE FINAL DAYS

By the last weekend of April, Ivan was back to driving but was not yet able to push Ian in his wheelchair. When we visited him, we did our routines and read Dr. Seuss books to him. And I always performed my repertoire on the keyboard. Ian looked paler and thinner, but he did not seem to be in any discomfort. He went to his day program whenever he could, but he began to refuse more of his meals and drink even less.

On Saturday, May 7th, we arranged for Ian to visit us along with a staff member. Without that extra help, we would not have been able to have Ian come to our house, since Ivan was still recovering from his surgery, and I just didn't have the strength to lift Ian in and out of his wheelchair. Staff always brought a light beanbag-type seat with them, since it gave Ian the support he needed and kept his legs in a position that didn't compromise his circulation. Ian enjoyed the music we played for him that day and ate the tuna fish sandwich Ivan prepared for him. On Sunday, Marsha and Steve visited him at River House. We had gotten into the habit of calling each other after our visits to Ian to report on his condition. When I got Marsha's call on Sunday afternoon, I was relieved that Ian was in a good mood, that he ate some of the sandwich she had brought for him, and drank his juice.

On Monday, Ian did not go to the day program. Although he ate his breakfast, he refused his lunch and dinner. Fran thought he seemed to be in pain, but he also refused to take his medication. The hospice nurse applied a patch for pain. Ivan and I went to River House on Tuesday morning. I didn't know whether Ian would rally once again as he had time after time. He drank some juice

    Harriet S. Mosatche

and had a bit of applesauce. He smiled when I sang and played on the keyboard and filled in words with gestures in his favorite Dr. Seuss books. But his gestures were more muted than usual. It was hard to leave him.

On Wednesday Ivan and I drove to Queens where I did a site visit for one of my evaluation projects and Ivan shopped for fruits and vegetables. We had planned to visit Ian on Thursday, but when Ivan picked me up after I had finished my work, he said that he had gotten a phone call, that Ian was not doing well. We drove to River House and went into Ian's room. His hospice aide Kenisha was with him as was another staff member. Ian had no color in his face, as if all the blood had left his body. He opened his eyes briefly, and I kissed him. I knew he was going to die soon. Tears filled my eyes, and I left the room to call Marsha. "We're at Ian's. You have to come here tonight. Ian is not going to last until tomorrow. I'll wait here for you." I thought about calling Jay but knew that he couldn't deal with the emotional pain of seeing Ian so close to death. Besides he rarely answered the phone, even when we used the code he had given to us to signal that the call would be from one of us.

I walked back to Ian's room and leaned over him. I kissed him and said: "You have been the most wonderful brother anyone could ever have. I love you very much and always will." Ivan, too, kissed Ian and told him the Willie Dreshen story for what, I knew, would be the last time. I called Robert and Elizabeth and put them on speaker phone so that Ian could hear their voices one more time. Kenisha left the room in tears. After a while, I went outside on the porch to wait for Marsha. When she arrived, we hugged and cried. I gave her and Steve time to be with Ian. I went back into Ian's room and kissed him again. I knew it would be the last time I would see Ian.

A few hours after returning home, the phone rang. I knew what the call was about before Ivan answered. Ian had just died, peacefully in his bed with Fran and two other staff with him. Ivan called Marsha, and then I talked to her for a while. We shared lots of tears and words of love. The hospice nurse called later on to say that Ian wore a beautiful smile.

CHAPTER 32

Saying Goodbye

The funeral took place on Friday, May 13, 2011, which gave Elizabeth time to get back to New York. Robert couldn't make it since he was in the middle of final exams at law school, and I assured him that he had been an incredible nephew and that's what counted. Rabbi Jo wasn't available to preside over the funeral, but one of her friends was. We decided to have a graveside service. Marsha's family was there, including Abigail. My friends Verna and Diane attended as did my cousin Rona and her daughters. Fran and several Richmond staff members came to say goodbye as well. Jay did not attend—going to funerals for those he loved was too difficult for him. After the rabbi recited a couple of traditional prayers and said a few words, several of us spoke, including staff members from River House. Marsha spoke first. I had told her I needed time to compose myself so I could speak about Ian.

MARSHA SAYS GOODBYE

This was Marsha's eulogy:

This is a very difficult day for me because I have to say a final goodbye to my brother Ian. He loved his family more than anything in the world. He loved me, his sister Harriet and his brother Jay so very, very much. His brother-in-laws Steve and Ivan were like real brothers to him. His nieces and nephews Sherry, Robert, Elizabeth and Ryan always

     Harriet S. Mosatche

cheered him up. When Ian met his great-niece Abigail, there was an instant connection. She would wave to him, and he would clap. Quite often, Abigail would point him out in the photo. She even asked for the album yesterday. She brought so much joy into his life and vice versa. Each of us knew how to make him happy. We all performed different skits for him. Ian always had a smile for all of us.

Ian had an extremely hard life. When he was born, his brain was deprived of oxygen and as a result, he was severely brain-injured. My parents did everything they could to give him a happy life. But at the age of 16, he was placed into an institution in Brooklyn where life was not good, to say the least. He was beaten and hospitalized many times. Finally, in the year 2000, he was placed in a wonderful group home where he remained until his death. His brother-in-law Ivan played a key role in getting Ian placed there. The staff and the residents all loved him. He will be greatly missed by all of them. Ian, I love you so much, and there will be a hole in my heart that only you can fill.

MY EULOGY

I spoke next, and hard as I tried, I couldn't stay composed throughout my eulogy. This is what I said that day:

Ian has always played such an important part in my life that I could write a book about it, and I might well do that. For now, I will just say that he helped me to understand what unconditional love is. Although his life was filled with challenges and very difficult times, he was also the epitome of pure joy. When I spent time with him, he made me feel that I was the most important person in the world. And when he smiled or laughed, he filled me with such happiness.

Who can I tell my Mr. Schmendrick story to now? Who can I talk about mature multi-vitamins to, using a bad

German accent? Who will appreciate me the way he did? I found my life's work because of him, and I will honor his memory by being as loving, caring, and patient as I can be.

Ivan was a brother to Ian, not a brother-in-law. And the compassion I now see in my children Liz and Rob was nourished by the time they spent with Ian. His life had an incredible impact on our family and those at his house and at Richmond who became part of his family and ours. I am grateful to everyone who made Ian's life as rich as it could be. My love for Ian will stay alive forever.

ELIZABETH'S SPECIAL DANCE

Elizabeth recited the following piece she wrote for Ian's funeral:

I've thought a lot in the last day and in the last few months about what Ian meant to me and how special and incredible he was. Back in December when things weren't looking so good, I talked to a friend about Ian and told her everything I could think of to tell her about him, to try to explain why I was so upset about what was going on. She was very sympathetic and comforting, but she didn't seem to entirely get it. When I was on the bus yesterday coming up from DC, I thought about everything I had told her and what I could've said to get her to truly understand Ian and my relationship with him. And I realized what I had left out. The reason thinking about him not being in my life anymore is so upsetting is that he made me feel special. The fact that I could make him smile, even on days when he seemed to be in a bad mood, made me feel important. Making him happy gave me such joy, and I was so proud that he had a symbol just for me. It's strange to think that no one will ever refer to me by tapping his foot anymore.

Dance is an important part of who I am, and it made me so happy to be able to share that with Ian and make

    Harriet S. Mosatche

him happy, and I think I felt most connected to him when I was dancing for him. On Wednesday night I got to talk to Ian on the phone and tell him I loved him, but I didn't fully realize until later that it was going to be the last time I talked to him, and I felt like I hadn't really gotten to say goodbye the way I wanted to. So before I went to bed I put on a song that I had listened to a lot in the past few months when I was feeling sad about what was going on with Ian or when I was worried about him. It's not one of his favorite songs—it's not "American Pie" or" Blue Suede Shoes"—it's probably not even a song he would like, but it made me feel connected to him anyway. And I put that song on and I danced to it. And when it was done I felt a little better; I felt like I had somehow said goodbye in my own way. That was probably around 10:45. I'm told that Ian passed at around 11 on Wednesday night. I know that the two are unrelated, but when I heard that I couldn't help but feel that maybe he had waited for me to say goodbye.

ROBERT AND IVAN RECITE A FINAL WILLIE DRESHEN STORY

Robert emailed his eulogy to us. It was based on the Willie Dreshen story that my father had told to Ian decades ago, and which had been told many, many times by others in the family. This is what Robert wrote, and Ivan recited with the right comic timing, but also with pauses when he was a bit overcome by emotion.

Ian was my uncle and I loved him. This is a variation on a story that my father and other relatives used to say to Ian when I was younger, and that, in recent years, it became my role to tell him.

When I was five years old, I went to kindergarten. One day (not the first day of class) my parents told me we were visiting my uncle Ian. I said: "What?" They said, "We're going to visit Ian. I said: "What?" They said: "We're going to visit Uncle Ian, get in the car and belt yourself." So I went to see Ian at BDC and I ran around inside the cafeteria and played basketball on the cracked courts all day, and I had a great time visiting him, but I still talked like this.

Then I went to first grade. On another day, also not the first day of class, my parents told me we were visiting my uncle Ian. I said: "What?" They said: "We're going to visit Ian. I said: "What?" They said: "We're going to visit Uncle Ian, get in the car and belt yourself." So I went to see Ian again at BDC, and I played on these odd contraptions that seemed to be like hamster exercise wheels for humans and explored all over the grounds, and I had a great time visiting him, but I still talked like this.

Then I was in 7ʰ grade, which for me was middle school, not junior high. One day, probably not long after the first day of class, my parents told me we were visiting my uncle Ian. I said: "What?" They said: "We're going to visit Ian. I said: "What?" They said: "We're going to visit Uncle Ian. get in the car and belt yourself." So I went to see Ian at BDC, and I ate lunch with my parents and sister, and my uncle Ian, and Uncle Jay, and Aunt Marsha and Uncle Steve, and cousins Sherry and Ryan, and I had a great time visiting Ian, but I still talked like this.

Then I went to high school, and not on the first day of class, I didn't get stuffed in a locker. Also, not on the first day of class, my parents told me we were visiting my uncle Ian. I said: "What? They said: "We're going to visit Ian. I said: "What?" They said: "We're going to visit Uncle Ian, get in the car and belt yourself." So I went to see Ian, this time at Richmond, and for the first time I told him the story of Wheelie Dreshen. I mixed it up a little bit because I couldn't remember all the lines, and I felt a little awkward telling him the story, but I had a great time visiting Ian. And even though I'd gone through puberty and didn't talk like I did before, I still talked like this.

 Harriet S. Mosatche

Then I went to college, and on the first day of class, I was far away from my family and Ian. But when I came home for winter break, my parents told me we were going to visit Ian. I said: "What?" They said: "We're going to visit Ian. I said: "What?" They said: "We're going to visit Uncle Ian, get in the car and belt yourself." So I went to see Ian at Richmond, and we took him outside and I pushed him up and down the street and told him the story of Wheelie Dreshen. I had it down now, but I threw in a different ending, because he seemed to like them, and although the girls still wouldn't dance with Wheelie, I had a great time visiting Ian, and I still talked like this.

Then I graduated from college, and went down to South America, and got a job and went to law school. And I didn't go to any graduation dance. But I did come home four weeks ago and saw an amazing, lovable man sitting in a bean bag chair at my house, so I went over to him and said: "Hey, Ian, wanna hear a story?" Ian said: "What?" I said: "I'm gonna tell you about Wheelie Dreshen. Listen up." So after I pushed Ian up and down the street, we stopped at the top of my parents' driveway, and Ian listened to me tell him about Wheelie Dreshen, and even though the girl still wouldn't dance with him, Ian smiled, and I had a great time visiting Ian, and I still talked like this.

Wednesday night, though, Ian passed away, and I won't be telling him the story of Wheelie Dreshen any longer, and I won't talk like this. But as it turns out Ian was never listening to me tell him the story of Wheelie Dreshen anyway, because as I just found out today, the man's name was Willie, and Ian was probably smiling and laughing because he thought I was an idiot for believing for 25 years that someone's name was actually Wheelie. But Willie, or Wheelie, or Ian, I think I've finally run out of clever reasons why the girl still wouldn't dance with you, so she's yours, Ian. I hope now you can talk however you want and dance the night away. I love you.

Epilogue

It has been more than eight years since Ian's death. On my desk is a piece of art Ian made for me. It's a smiley face made with buttons, glitter, and ribbon glued to a piece of tin. The montage of photos of Ian along with captions that staff at River House framed for me stayed hidden for almost a year. It was too painful to see Ian's smiling face and his familiar gestures. Finally, I hung it in the basement so I could look at it from time to time. Marsha has a framed photo of herself with Ian in her dining room. Recently, she said that she might move the photo—it still makes her sad although it is a beautiful portrait that reflects the love between siblings. Although Marsha and I talk about wanting to visit River House, we have not gone back since the memorial service held two weeks after Ian's death when a lilac bush was planted in Ian's memory. For a while I saved a stack of O magazines to give to Susan. Since we didn't return to River House, Marsha now gets my copies. Tom's sister wrote to us to express her condolences. "It will be so odd to walk into River House and not see Ian. I am sure you are missing him every day. We do miss him, too."

A couple of months after Ian's death, I received an email from Jane, the former Richmond staff member who had been instrumental in getting Ian out of BDC and into River House. She said that doing that was a highlight of her career. Rabbi Jo and I communicated by email for a while, and her messages have always meant a lot to me. When she asked Ivan and me to present at a hospice conference she was coordinating, we were glad to talk to professionals in the field about our personal journey with Ian. Rabbi Jo was able to preside at the unveiling service we held for Ian about a year after his death. Elizabeth, Robert, Sherry, Marsha, Annie, and I all spoke. Kaleigh left a bachelorette party in Boston early so she

 Harriet S. Mosatche

could join our family at this service. I am happy that the woman Robert married got to know Ian well enough that she cried when she learned he had died.

At the unveiling, Marsha talked about how important Ian was to her, how he changed her life in many ways. She spoke to him directly when she said: "You made me stronger, more confident, and more compassionate." Sherry talked about the bond that had developed between her daughter Abigail and Ian. And she noted that "because of Uncle Ian, I have a strong sensitivity to people with disabilities." Although I told Annie that she didn't need to come down from Boston, she and her boyfriend made the trip for the unveiling. I really would have understood if she couldn't make it, but when she said that she "had to be there," I was pleased with her decision. She talked about her memories of Ian and how she had learned from him about the true meaning of family, patience, and acceptance.

I spoke about the book I was writing, which didn't have a title yet, and I said: "Ian's story is one that needs to be told, to demonstrate vividly that a life of severe disability is still an important life...I believe that Ian's life influenced the way Ivan, Robert, and Elizabeth live their lives and that the cycle will continue with those whose lives they touch."

Elizabeth hadn't prepared anything formal, but her eloquence in describing how much Ian meant to her touched me in a deep way. She described the charity race that she, Robert, and Kaleigh had run in the day before, an event to raise money for people with developmental disabilities. My brother had left his fingerprints on Elizabeth's heart, too.

Robert said:

The Wheelie Dreshen story began every part with 'When I was five years old' or 'When I went to college.' Well, when I was 25 years old, my uncle Ian passed away and I've missed him ever since. It hasn't been how I expected it to be. When

Several months after Ian's death, Jay fell while walking back from the grocery store and shattered his shoulder. Ivan took him to the emergency room, and the doctor told Jay that he needed surgery. At the pre-op procedures, we learned that Jay had major damage to his heart, evidently sustained in a past heart attack. Jay refused to consider the cardiac surgery that was required before his shoulder could be operated on, and he returned home. Marsha and I were unable to convince him to see a cardiologist, but we (with our husbands) visited him more often to help him with chores. By August of 2013, Jay's health had deteriorated so much that he finally agreed to go to the emergency room of a local hospital. He stayed in the hospital for two weeks; we found out that he was suffering from congestive heart failure with his heart functioning at about 15 percent of capacity with a clot in a heart chamber. After five weeks in a cardiac rehab facility, Jay returned to his apartment with a full medicine regimen that he followed religiously. Sadly, Ivan and I found him dead on the floor near the door of his apartment when we went to visit him to refill his medicine containers in February 2014. Another younger brother to bury and mourn.

Marsha became a grandmother a second time soon after Jay's death. Abigail and Sophia bring her incredible joy. However, she is a bit sad that Abigail no longer remembers Ian and their powerful bond—she was just too young when he died.

                      Harriet S. Mosatche

Seven years after Ian's death, Elizabeth received her Ph.D. and became Dr. Lawner, as Ian knew she would be. She works as a research director at a start-up educational company. She married Jon, an emergency room physician, in 2017. How we could have used his help with all the injuries and illnesses Ian had.

Robert, who graduated from law school in 2013, spent several months while still in school working as a research assistant for a lawyer who was writing a book about funding for people with disabilities. Robert moved back to New York to join a law firm after a year in Austin as a law clerk to a federal appeals court judge. He married Kaleigh in 2015, and in 2019, they had a child Charlee—our first grandchild. Kaleigh works as a speech and language pathologist with preschoolers who have autism.

Unfortunately, the kidney disease that took Ian's life is now part of mine. I am hoping to get a transplant before I need to go on dialysis, but so far, no family member or friend has been a match or passed the health tests to become a donor. Ivan retired from practicing law. He was disappointed to learn that not only was he not a match for me, but he didn't pass the health screening that would have allowed him to be part of a kidney exchange that would have given me a kidney.

I learned from a February 1, 2015 article in the *New York Times* that the Brooklyn Developmental Center was to close by the end of that year. That article featured a man who had spent 36 years at that facility, and although there was a photo of him, I didn't recognize his face. However, the pictures of the grounds and main building looked all too familiar. I was struck by the $625,000 settlement that the Consentino family received in 2010 when the center "did not properly diagnose John's tooth access and treat his self-injurious behavior with antipsychotic medication." Ian's tardy diagnoses and numerous injuries caused by neglect were probably worth many millions. But that's the past, and what's important to me now is telling about Ian's life so that the fingerprints left by his life provide impetus for discussion and change in how people with disabilities and their families are perceived and treated in our society. Since the election of Donald Trump as president in 2016, I have become more concerned that our country is turning back to the intolerance that marked Ian's growing up years. During the campaign when Trump made fun of a reporter's disability, I shuddered. And when Trump's Secretary of Education talks about making changes that will no longer protect the rights of those with disabilities, I am frightened that instead of moving forward we are going backwards. Ian's fingerprints remain on my heart, and they continue to propel me to advocate for acceptance and respect for those who are like him.

As a final personal note, Ivan and I have incorporated the expressions Ian loved into our everyday conversation. "Toooo late" from the Mr. Schmendrick story is one phrase others might hear us say when we've forgotten to get an item from Costco or realized that a CVS coupon had expired before we could use it. And we laugh, just as Ian did.

 Harriet S. Mosatche